D1219468

MEZE

Appetizers & Petite Plates

Kukla's KOUZINA

A Gourmet Journey~Greek Island Style

MEZE

Appetizers & Petite Plates

By Kelly Salonica Staikopoulos with Joanne Staikopoulos Marzella

Recipes by Mary Halkias Staikopoulos, Kelly Salonica Staikopoulos,
and Joanne Staikopoulos Marzella

Kukla's Kouzina: A Gourmet Journey-Greek Island Style, Meze
Author: Kelly Salonica Staikopoulos
Publisher: Kukla's Kouzina, LLC

Copyright © 2018 by Kelly Salonica Staikopoulos

Text and interior photographs copyright © 2018 by Kelly Salonica Staikopoulos.
Cover photograph copyright © 2018 by Anastassios Mentis. Interior photographs
copyright © 2018 by Anastassios Mentis, Kelly Salonica Staikopoulos, Joanne
Staikopoulos Marzella, and Jacqueline Maria Marzella. Map on page 6 courtesy of
the Pan-Karpathian Foundation.

All rights reserved. No part of this book may be reproduced or utilized in any
manner whatsoever without the prior written permission from the publisher
except in the case of brief quotations embodied in critical articles and reviews.
For information address Kukla's Kouzina, LLC, PO Box 223, Valhalla, New York
10595-0223 or contact thegirls@kuklaskouzina.com.

Kukla's Kouzina and design are registered trademarks of Kelly Staikopoulos and
Joanne Marzella.

Library of Congress Control Number: 2018948016
Staikopoulos, Kelly
        Kukla's kouzina : A gourmet journey-Greek island style,
            meze / Kelly Salonica Staikopoulos with Joanne
            Staikopoulos Marzella ; photographs by Anastassios
            Mentis, Kelly Salonica Staikopoulos, Joanne Staikopoulos
            Marzella, and Jacqueline Maria Marzella
        1st ed. p. cm.
        Includes biographical references and index.
        ISBN 978-0-9982395-0-7
        1. Cookery, Greek. 2. Food habits, Greece. I. Title.

Text by Kelly Salonica Staikopoulos
Cover design by Nancy Karamarkos
Cover photograph by Anastassios Mentis
Photographs (interior) by Anastassios Mentis, Kelly Salonica Staikopoulos,
        Joanne Staikopoulos Marzella, and Jacqueline Maria Marzella
Book design by Nancy Karamarkos
Contributing designer: Ann Kielbasa
Food styling by Kelly Salonica Staikopoulos
Prop styling by Nancy Karamarkos and Kelly Salonica Staikopoulos
Copy editor/editor: Mark Amundsen
Cover photograph: Mini Cheese Pies with Homemade Dough
        (Tyropitakia me Spitiko Fillo), page 26

Published and printed in the United States of America

First Edition

1 2 3 4 5 6 7 8 9 10

www.kuklaskouzina.com

For Kukla, our mom Mary, who blessed us with her eternal love and taught us about food, Karpathian culture, and our family history. All the magic between these pages unfolded in the heart of our home, our *kouzina*.

APELLA BEACH

CONTENTS

ACKNOWLEDGMENTS vii
FOREWORD xi
INTRODUCTION 1
KARPATHOS: An Island of Mythological Proportions 7
PREPARATION: Go Greek Cooking 101...*the Basics!* 11
MEZE: Appetizers & Petite Plates 12

SPREADS & DIPS 13
Lemon-Pepper Hummus (*Houmous me Lemoni kai Piperi*)
(Variations: Sun-dried Tomato Hummus,
Olive Hummus, Artichoke and Spinach Hummus)
Olive Paste/Spread (*Pasta Elias*)
Yogurt-Cucumber Sauce/Dip (*Tzatziki*)
Garlic Sauce/Dip (*Skordalia*)
Carp (fish) Roe Spread (*Taramosalata*)
Eggplant-Salad Spread (*Melitzanosalata*)

PASTRIES 21
Spinach Puffs (*Spanaki Sfoliata*)
Olive Puffs (*Elia Sfoliata*)
Mini Cheese Pies with Homemade Dough (*Tyropitakia me Spitiko Fillo*)
Cheese Rolls (*Mbourekia me Tyri*)
Meat Rolls (*Mbourekia me Kima*)
Phyllo Cheese Triangles (*Tyropitakia Trigona me Fillo*)

PETITE PLATES 31
Fried Greek Cheese Flambé (*Saganaki*)
Greek Shrimp Cocktail (*Garides me Saltsa Kokteil*)
Stuffed Mushrooms (*Gemista Manitaria*)
Ham Canapés (*Kanape me Zampon*)
Cocktail Meatballs (*Keftedakia*)
Stuffed Grape Leaves (*Dolmadakia me Klimatofilla*)
Meatless-Lenten Stuffed Grape Leaves (*Dolmadakia Gialantzi-Nistisima*)

GREEK COOKING TECHNIQUES 43
KOUZINA A TO Ω: Equipment, Ingredients, Common
Cooking Methods & Food Terms of Greek Island Cuisine 47
GREEK FOOD & PRODUCT SOURCES 62
INDEX 64
ABOUT THE AUTHOR & THE TEAM 66
ABOUT KUKLASKOUZINA.COM 67

ACKNOWLEDGMENTS

First to our Kukla, our mom, for her cherished recipes that bring back timeless memories, allowing us to revisit precious moments, and for her enormous love that will never die. Her lessons in our *kouzina* taught us about our roots, made us appreciate our time with her, and laid a foundation for us to continue to create new recipes in the traditions we share. Our mom's most valuable lesson was that through God all things are possible, and we are thankful for His many gifts!

FROM KELLY

To four generations of women who momentously inspired my life:
To my *yiayia*, Kalliope—for whom I was named—although we never met, I know you in my heart and soul and profoundly thank you for sending your love from above, for keeping a journal of your recipes, for passing down the foodie genes, and, more importantly, for giving us the gift of our mom, Mary, our "Kukla."

To my mom, Mary (Kukla), thank you for your immeasurable offering of unconditional love, for the delicious life you shared with us, and for your perpetual faith in me. I miss you every moment of every day! A special thanks, Mom, for the best gift you ever gave me, my sister, Joanne.

To my sister, Joanne, God made us sisters, but hearts made us friends. You not only rolled up your sleeves and helped test our recipes, you developed some of your own to enhance our collection. We shared laughter making videos and put our heads together to get a recipe to work when it gave us a hard time testing it on our own. Thanks for the love and the journey, and for the gift of my niece, Jackie.

To my niece, Jackie, our next generation, thanks for embodying the spirit of your grandma Mary, for always wanting to cook and bake alongside us, for your creative input, and for the love you always share. I couldn't be more proud of the lovely young lady you've become. You are a gift I will forever treasure.

To friends:
To rock-star sales coach, speaker, and author Mj Callaway for your direction, advice, and counseling. To fellow writer Kris Wetherbee for your loving encouragement, support, Facebook shares, and Twitter #FFFs. Girlfriends, you make

my heart sing songs of gladness! To Pam Vu and Johnny Wong for your InDesign and tech support; you helped me make sense of the tools I needed to finish this project. My sanity thanks you! To Monique Gaudin for your faith and "I'm so proud of you" notes. To Joni Strandquest for your marketing expertise. To Steve Cook for always promoting this project. To Maria Lisella for the social media shares and publishing advice. Thank you all for your editorial contributions and cheers from the sidelines, but most of all I'm grateful for your friendships! To fellow Karpathian Irene Gounaris of Omega Wines & Spirits for your enthusiasm and praise for this project, and your vision for its greatness.

Thanks to all my wonderful friends and fellow food bloggers I met through Foodify on Facebook and Twitter. Your support and love are very much appreciated. A special thanks to Panayiotis Galanis for your social media expertise—I thought I had it covered but learned that, with the right guide, there's always room for improvement.

Many thanks to the *Ladies' Home Journal* food department dream-team (1997 to 2001), Jan Hazard, Carol Prager, Cynthia DePersio, Regina Ragone, Sarah Platt White, and Jane Yagoda-Goodman, for teaching me the skills of food editing and recipe testing that prepared me for the journey ahead, and for including me in your "family." Having the privilege of working with all of you made my time at *LHJ* an experience I will always hold dear.

FROM JOANNE

To family past and present:

To my *papou*, Ioannis—for whom I was named and was blessed to spend the first nine years of my life with—from the moment you shared your *psomi* (bread) dunked in your *kafe* (coffee) with me, I became a lover of food pairing...and coffee! You stretched out your loving hand to help raise Kelly and me, and we will remember you always.

To my *yiayia*, Kalliope, while you were taken from us far too soon, you will never be forgotten. You left behind a cherished food legacy that paved the way to this cookbook. Thank you for the gift of our mom, our Kukla, who carried on your legacy, built on it, and passed it down to us.

To Mom, Kukla—who was just that, a *kukla* (doll)—who was loving and compassionate. You constantly sacrificed for Kelly and me, and taught us everything we know about cooking, especially when it comes to Greek island cuisine. You were ever-present in our daily lives and now your absence is felt each moment. We were blessed to have you as a mom, friend, and mentor, and you are missed every day.

To my sister, Kelly, I appreciate and love you more than words can express. You have a gift for writing and baking that cannot be matched. This book would never have happened if not for your talents, perseverance, and positive attitude. Sometimes they say you can't pick your relatives...I couldn't have picked better!

To my husband, Vinnie, thank you for your love and support through all the recipe testing and photo shoots. Thank you for all the advice, especially the tax counseling. I love you.

To my daughter, Jackie, you challenge me every day to be a better person and mom. From the age of two-and-a-half you always wanted to cook alongside me and change the recipes. You have your *yiayia* Mary's touch and I pray you never let it go. You are and always will be in my heart.

To friends:

To Father Elias Villis and George Hazlaris for your spiritual guidance, friendship, and for teaching me that through Christ all things are possible.

To Craig Penn for all your legal advice and support, we are so grateful. To Susan Papacostas and Harriet Tolve for your thoughtful counsel. To Chrys Simos, thank you for your skilled review of our Greek text, and for your friendship.

To Helen Kier, Kathy Staten, Joni Alexopoulos, Elizabeth Vallas Kreder, Pamela Smith, Audrey Blauner, and Lori Sparano for your continual support to both of us—I know you are all just a phone call away when we need you. We are so blessed to have such incredible friends.

Our lives have been blessed and enriched with the most amazing friends whose abilities, support, and encouragement have made this cookbook possible, allowing us to soar to magnificent heights.

Our heartfelt gratitude to our dear friends, art director Nancy Karamarkos and photographer Anastassios Mentis, who beautified our book and project. To Nancy for designing our gorgeous cover, book, and logo—the motifs capture the essence of our mom's taste and we know she gives them her blessing. To Anastassios for making our foods look as good as they taste. Thank you both for the immense generosity of your time and talents. Agape!

To Ann Kielbasa, we thank you for your design assistance.

To our dear friend Mark Amundsen for gifting us with his proficient research, editing, and copyediting skills. Editors don't receive enough praise for what they do. Mark, we're so glad you have our backs! You make us look good while keeping us smiling. And to Mark's wife, Tracy, who came up with the perfect phrase when we couldn't express an emotion into words...you gave voice to our hearts with your rare gift of intuition.

Most importantly, our thanks go out to our mom and grandmother who kept records of their recipes, and taught each generation about the culture and traditions embodied in this unique and delectable cuisine. The seeds they planted over the years sprouted into the roots of this cookbook, and brought forth the development of some of our own recipes that have emerged from our vital training. The result is a series of cookbooks we're tremendously proud of and happy to be sharing after our long journey from inception to completion.

FOREWORD

Kukla's Kouzina: A Gourmet Journey~Greek Island Style, Meze is unlike any Greek or Mediterranean cookbook that has ever been published. This is because of our approach and substance, both of which are equally important to its uniqueness. Meze recipes for holidays and year-round celebrations, as well as every day, make this an appetizer cookbook for all seasons.

Like our mom's inspiration from the island of Karpathos, *Kukla's Kouzina* is enticing, delicious, rich, vibrant, inspiring, and at once a piece of evolving history, a life-renewing force, and an eternal tribute to the magical talents of the woman who made it all possible.

As Kukla always signed off her recipes, we wish you

Kali orexi!

Καλή όρεξη!

Good appetite!

—KELLY SALONICA STAIKOPOULOS

Clockwise from top left: Kukla's family when she (far right) was only four; Kukla (right) with designer Carolyne Roehm at her Holiday party showing off Kukla's seasonally-decorated *tourta amigdalou* (almond torte) and Greek cookies; Aunt Frances in our Brooklyn Heights kitchen (circa 1950s) making *karidopita* (syruped walnut cake); Kukla with Oscar de la Renta on her birthday.

INTRODUCTION

OUR KUKLA

She studied design and was the sought-after sample cutter who helped create the most talked-about runway vogues that positioned her to fit the likes of supermodels, celebrities, politician's wives, and the wealthy elite. Known as "Mary the Greek" for more than three decades up and down New York City's Seventh Avenue by most of the fashion industry's top designers she assisted—including Halston, Carolina Herrera, Vera Wang, Donna Karan, Oscar de la Renta, and Oleg Cassini—Mary Halkias Staikopoulos was more affectionately called "Kukla," the Greek word for a *doll* used to describe a beautiful woman, by those closest to her. She first bestowed this nickname on all of her "girls," the ladies she worked with, and she ultimately became *their* doll as well. It was a term of endearment that we all adopted. To us, Kukla was our teacher, our inspiration, and our much-adored mom.

OUR KOUZINA

Our "kouzina," the Greek word for *kitchen*, was where our admiration for superb food was born and where we learned to appreciate our mom's unique way with cooking, Greek island style! Mom was often told by the designers and professionals she knew, such as Carolyne Roehm, that she could make a fortune going into the food business, and was asked numerous times why she never opened her own restaurant. With her two brothers having done just that, and seeing the backbreaking hours they put into it, she knew this course was not for her. Though becoming a professional chef was not her choice, the idea of taking on the role of cookbook author played somewhere in the back of her mind.

Our mom, like her mother before her, kept two handwritten notebooks of her recipes—one for savory dishes and one for sweets—and, through trial and error, worked them to perfection. She made a vocation out of reinventing recipes and wasn't satisfied with anything less than the best. Her talent for design and her flair for the dramatic made everything as beautiful on the outside as it was on the inside. Our *kouzina* was where we watched it all unfold.

OUR JOURNEY

The concept for this journey began with Mom's passion for the art of cooking. She possessed the innate skill to take dishes to their highest potential, a talent she inherited from *her* mother, Kalliope, who was born and raised in Volada, a hillside village on the Dodecanese island of Karpathos in Greece.

Mom was first-generation American, born the third child of four in Richland, West Virginia, to a coal miner (formerly a marble miner in Greece and Egypt) and a mother who took pride in how she raised her family. At the age of six, seated at the dinner table, Mom was served *fava*, a bowl of thick yellow split-pea soup drizzled with lemon juice and olive oil—a dish she refused to eat. She never had it before but decided she didn't like it. Most kids these days would get away with finicky eating while their mothers scramble to heat up canned soup or chicken fingers, but *this* child, our mom, was in for a rude awakening. Her mother said if she wasn't going to eat she was to excuse herself and go to bed. It ended up being an early night for Mom. The following day, while everyone else enjoyed a Greek roast-chicken dinner, the same plate of *fava* was placed in front of our mom. Again she refused and it was off to bed. Her father, our *papou* (grandfather), began to object: "You can't send the child to bed hungry again!" to which her mother, our *yiayia* (grandmother) tossed back, in typical old-world Greek fashion, "You go work and bring home the money and *I'll* raise the kids!" On the third night the *fava* was back in front of Mom. By then she was so hungry that she not only ate all of it, wiping the plate clean with a piece of crusty bread, but discovered it was good and asked for more. Yiayia's *fava*-fast was a bit extreme but it worked, and it sent out a message to all the kids that dictating what was on the menu was *her* job, not theirs—learning how to eat started at home.

That early lesson opened the door to a world of culinary delights for our mom, one that she would share with us. We never went through the *fava*-fast, but we did grow up with a healthy curiosity for food, trying and enjoying just about everything Mom cooked or baked...and so did everyone else who was fortunate enough to know her!

While our *papou* worked the coal mines in Wheeling, our *yiayia* was busy bribing his foreman with Karpathian food and sweets so he wouldn't send Papou deep into the dangerous tunnels. She was frugal with his earnings, and once she saved up enough money, she told Papou that he was done with the mines and she was done worrying about him. She then announced to the family that they were going into the restaurant business. Our uncles, teenagers at the time, laughed at her, saying that she didn't know anything about American food so there was no way she could make it work. Well, that's all she needed to hear. Our *yiayia* told her sons that making chili dogs and meatloaf would be easy to figure out after cooking Greek all her life. Her chili, roast turkey, and brisket were just a few of the items on the menu, plus she would throw in some *spanakopita*, *souvlaki*, *moussaka*, and *avgolemono* soup to make their eatery unique...and, near their home in Charleston, the Busy Bee diner was born.

Our *yiayia's* talent for making food, and her speed in its preparation, made the diner a huge success—and this same talent and skill was passed on to our mom, who amazed us each time she quickly whipped up something outstanding. For our uncles, this first restaurant experience was the foundation for a lifetime in the business, ultimately landing them in New York City's Little Italy with their own luncheonette.

Our mother moved to New York at the age of eighteen to become a designer. She studied at the prestigious Traphagen School of Fashion, the Fashion Institute of Technology (FIT), and Parsons School of Design. But her dreams took a detour—not only with two young children to raise on her own, but also financial hardships following a narrow escape from an abusive marriage. She always wanted to have children and, for her, all other desires paled in comparison. Though difficult times were her constant companion, she made sure we remained blissfully content.

Mom took her training in design and reshaped her career to become a successful sample cutter for some of the top fashion designers in New York City. Marilyn Monroe, a client of Oleg Cassini's (Mom worked on her wardrobe as well as those of Rose and Jacqueline Kennedy), remarked that Mom's light-as-air spinach pie was "absolutely wonderful." When Mom arrived with her Christmas cookies and *tourta amigdalou* (almond torte) at Carolyne Roehm's annual yuletide party, an elaborate affair prepared by Carolyne's personal chef, Carolyne announced that her "table is now complete!" Kevan Hall, the last designer she worked with at Halston (and a guest judge on *America's Next Top Model*), said, "She brought life into our otherwise dismal showroom gifting us with her laughter, dance, and fabulous food." Year after year, these designers requested her captivating entrées and irresistible cookies for their holiday parties, and they were highly favored for good reason.

Mom was the master in our *kouzina*, and there wasn't one thing she didn't know how to cook when it came to Greek and Karpathian food.

Our earliest and fondest memory of cooking, or in this case baking, was at the ages of four and five when our mom sat us down on a frosty December morning to make our Christmas cookies, the very same ones that she took to Carolyne Roehm's parties. These weren't just any cookies. They were Greek, which translated into us learning techniques such as rolling, filling, and decorating for three different kinds of cookies: *melomakarona* (also known as *finikia*), *kourambiedes*, and *koulourakia*. And we weren't making just a few dozen; it was two hundred of each kind. These cookies were so special that our mom would package them up with pretty silk bows and give them as Christmas gifts to friends and co-workers every year—they were eagerly anticipated and seriously appreciated. By the time we were in high school we realized why she got us started so young—she needed the help!

The first cookie we learned how to make was *koulourakia*. The idea was to roll out each piece of dough into a perfect rope before twisting it. In the beginning we repeatedly asked Mom, "How come we can't do it?" We were frustrated because her ropes always looked so flawless and ours were skinny on one side and lumpy in the middle. She was infinitely patient with us and explained that this dough needs to be worked well (thoroughly kneaded) before rolling, then she had us start at the center of the rope, rolling it gently out to the ends. She said the more we practiced and got a feel for the dough, the better our cookies would look, and the easier it would get. This is how she learned from *her* mom.

While we rolled and shaped and twisted, Mom shared stories about how Yiayia and Papou met in Karpathos, at the altar—it was an arranged marriage, courtesy of our great-grandmother, when Yiayia was just fifteen. We learned about the Karpathian foods Yiayia grew up cooking that prepared her to run her own household. We discovered that our great-grandmother was a midwife and since there was no doctor on the island, she was regarded as the go-to physician for any and all ailments, as well as for birthing babies. Mom told us about her family growing up in West Virginia, Athens, and Karpathos. She recalled Papou's coal-mine days, her *fava*-fast, and Yiayia saving up to open the Busy Bee. She shared her teenage dreams of becoming a designer that took her from apprenticing with a furrier in West Virginia to attending the most prestigious design school in New York City, and how those dreams were deflected and replaced with children, and how that far surpassed her life's expectations.

It was during this shared time with Mom in our *kouzina* that we learned more than just how to make cookies. We learned about our heritage and customs. Our mom was laying down a foundation that we could build on.

When Mom felt that we put enough time into making the *koulourakia*, she gave us each a piece of dough to roll out and cut into Christmas shapes like trees, camels, and stars...this was the part we loved! We'd sprinkle our cookies with red and green sugar and bake them alongside our mom's twists. The smell coming from the oven was heaven and it ushered in Christmastime.

This annual tradition has withstood the test of time, and today we're experts at making *koulourakia* and all of the cookies—yes, practice does make perfect—and we taught my niece, Jackie (Mom's granddaughter), the same way our mom taught us. We knock out six hundred cookies in a two-day marathon, and Jackie is always eager to get started. In fact, Jackie has been our official sugar-duster and nut-sprinkler since she was four—and she gets her own piece of dough to cut out and decorate just like we did. Plus we never have to worry about over-baking—from the moment Jackie could speak she's been shouting out *"COOKIES!"* whenever the oven timer goes off...just in case we didn't hear it. Like our Kukla, we distribute them to family, friends, and co-workers who eagerly await their arrival each year—it's the official start of the holiday season for excited recipients, and a gift that's always prized.

When we were about six, our *theia* Franghi (aunt Frances) was baking bread—Yiayia's recipe for *Christopsomo* (Christ's Bread)—and as soon as she took it out of the oven we were begging for a taste. She told us that she couldn't cut the bread until it cooled a bit, otherwise it would be too wet on the inside. Each time she baked, we asked the same question and got the same response. One night, while the fifteen-inch round loaf was cooling, the aroma was so intense that we couldn't wait. We devised a plan. While our mom and aunt were busy in the living room, we went into the kitchen and poked a couple of holes in the side of the loaf and pulled out some of the crumb. We turned the bread so our handiwork was hidden, ate our booty, and went to watch TV. Later on we overheard our aunt telling our mother that she thought we had mice...actually *two* mice that got into the bread via perfectly round holes. The jig was up. We were disappointed to discover that we weren't as clever as we thought!

The art of bread-making so intrigued me that Theia taught me how to make *Christopsomo* when I was ten years old, and I've been baking it ever since. Passing on the bread-making tradition must be an aunt-niece thing, because I introduced it to Jackie when she was just two and a half—we were speechless when we saw her instinctively kneading it like her grandma Mary.

When we were little, our *yiayia's* handwritten cookbook, which contained the *Christopsomo* recipe, was lost. One day, many years later, while looking through some family documents with Mom, we found the cookbook (dating back to the 1920s) and it was better than discovering gold! The only problem was that Yiayia wasn't formally schooled, so she wrote as she heard, in sentences that were just a single run-on word. The only way for us to decipher her recipes was to enunciate them out loud—a process that often turned frustration into laughter. The considerable time it took to decipher her recipes was definitely time well spent!

Baking has always been one of my passions, so when it came to making bread, decorating a cake, or jazzing up a piecrust for a pita, I was assigned that duty by the boss, Mom! While I was busy making bread, Joanne was helping Mom make stuffed tomatoes and peppers. She remembers Mom telling her that she had to break up the ground beef for the filling with the back of a wooden spoon (Yiayia's spoon, actually) while browning it, until the texture was really fine...no lumps allowed! I still have that spoon and use it every time I brown ground beef. That was the first step in making a filling that had the perfect consistency. This technique was the basis for many of Mom's recipes, including her meat sauce, *moussaka*, *pastitsio*, and so much more. Once you mastered it, you were ready to make it all!

While bread, pastries, and desserts are my forte, Joanne's love of cooking led to her inventive re-creation of some of Mom's recipes into vegetarian/Lenten versions, while also providing a number of tasty fasting options. Following her mom's example, Jackie has embarked on re-creating her grandma Mary's recipes into dairy-free versions for those who are sensitive to dairy, as she is. As a result, the most-requested recipes that we created and perfected will appear alongside Kukla's in various editions of this cookbook series.

TGIF meant more to us than just the end of the school week. Friday was the day Mom would come home with bags of gourmet goodies from Ninth Avenue in Manhattan's Hell's Kitchen. After work she'd head over to Esposito's for the finest meats and International Grocery for feta, kasseri cheese, olives, and all foods Greek (the Karamouzis brothers have owned the market for decades and still run it). She then checked out which market had the freshest fish and picked out artisan bread from the local bakery. Carrying bags weighing about fifty pounds in each hand (we joked with her that she was "strong like bull!"), she braved the subway and headed home. Joanne and I waited for Mom on the stoop of our brownstone and ran to her as soon as we spotted her coming down our block. We were so happy she was home, and she was visibly thrilled to see us, resulting in hugs and kisses all around. Nights following a Ninth Avenue run meant we were having fresh ham-and-feta heroes with lettuce and tomato, all the ingredients from the treasures found in Mom's shopping bags. She used to ask us not to tell anyone we were eating sandwiches for dinner, which we couldn't understand, because we thought this was the best meal ever!

When it came to entertaining, be it *Pascha* (Easter), Thanksgiving, Christmas, birthdays, or a dinner party, Mom was busily preparing, running back and forth between the kitchen and the dining room, and making sure her guests had everything they needed. She was always the last one to sit down at the table and she encouraged everyone to start eating without her so the food wouldn't get cold. For Mom it was about the serving and creating a memorable evening. Her guests would tell her that dinner at Kukla's was like going to a five-star restaurant. One night it was fruit-salad flambé served as a first course—Mom always stressed that just because you're serving a salad doesn't mean it has to be ordinary, an opinion clearly demonstrated in her fish-shaped tuna salad complete with sliced-carrot scales and olive eyes. Another occasion, it began with Greek Shrimp Cocktail (page 34) arranged in scooped out pineapple halves.

Mom taught us that our focus should be on great cuisine *and* its dazzling presentation—every day was a celebration of life and food!

The example she set took root when we were about ten and decided to surprise Mom with an exotic meal when she came home from work, giving her a break from cooking that night. It was a Greek luau...yes, I said "*Greek* luau"! We prepared our mom's lemon chicken and potatoes recipe (using Cornish hens) and roasted the meal in an oven bag. While that was roasting, we tossed a Greek salad, then cut the tops off of pineapples and scooped out the insides. We filled the pineapples with fruit juice and topped each with a cherry-and-pineapple-skewered cocktail umbrella. We cut up the rest of the pineapple, combined it with other fruit, and served it for dessert. We spread out a blanket on our kitchen floor and set it with the pineapple drinks, tropical flowers, paper plates, napkins, and plastic utensils (so there was no dish washing that night either).

As soon as we heard her come up the stairs we turned down the lights and turned on the Hawaiian music to set the mood. We greeted her with a lei that matched the ones we were wearing. She was beyond surprised—she was deeply touched and so proud of us. Not only did her young girls prepare dinner, but they had also made an elaborate, creative effort that was inspired by love and the standard she set for us. Though she wasn't the type to eat on the floor, she did it because we went to all the trouble and she didn't want us to feel bad. She quickly got over the seating arrangements and we had the best time. Each course was an *"Oh my goodness, look at what you did!"* moment for her. We ate, we laughed, and we made a very special memory that warmed all of our hearts for years to come, especially today, when those memories are so precious.

We lived in a home abundant in love, laughter, and the familiar smell of something delicious being prepared in the kitchen. As tired as Mom was when she got home from work and school, cooking was never a chore and dinner was always extraordinary! Eating well was her first priority for us and food was something she didn't skimp on. She was our hero and her lessons were invaluable. Having Kukla as our mom? Now *that* was priceless!

We started writing this cookbook series with our mother in 1997. Unfortunately, she was diagnosed with cancer one year later. In the year before her diagnosis an ominous feeling compelled us to learn not only how to read her Greek script, a challenge to be sure, but also to record measurement amounts for typical Greek recipe terms like *a handful*, *1 wineglass*, and *1 water glass*—the most daunting being *1 little plastic cup*. Since there's no standard for all of these measurements (as each glass or cup comes in a different size), we sat her down and had her show us which vessels she used, then filled them with water and emptied each into a measuring cup to get an accurate reading. Without the insight to do this one simple thing, these recipes would have been impossible to re-create. In that one year we learned all her secrets, which directed us to a vision for a cookbook...*her* cookbook.

Though our mom didn't survive to see the cookbook completed, the dream that was born in our Brooklyn Heights kitchen so many years ago still lives on. Her handwritten recipes (some dating back to the 1950s), along with a few of our grandmother's (dating back as far as the 1920s), most of which we translated from Greek, and a few of our own drawn from our experience cooking with our mom side-by-side from the ages of four and five, have given us the tools to make this dream a reality.

Together we learned that cooking truly keeps our family memories alive. This is our Kukla's legacy, a collection of timeless recipes that will bring new excitement to Greek cuisine and will instruct the average cook precisely how to make extraordinary meals and sumptuous treats.

Kukla's handwritten *Tyropitakia* recipe (page 26)

This cookbook series celebrates more than fifteen years of labor and discovery—the physical process of writing it and the awakening of our cultural roots, which we had long forgotten. Our time between then and now has been spent translating the recipes, testing them until they work perfectly, editing them so they're easy to understand and reproduce, and finally developing some of our own recipes that are rooted in the traditions we were taught. Each recipe features its proper Greek name as an acknowledgement to our heritage, as well as its English translation. We learned that the common thread for all of us is food, and the love and history it epitomizes. The result—a recipe collection and a companion website and blog—is an accomplishment we're tremendously proud of and happy to be sharing after our long journey from inception to completion.

—KELLY

KARPATHOS

AN ISLAND OF MYTHOLOGICAL PROPORTIONS

Let the warm Mediterranean breeze fill your sails and prepare to be taken on a delectable voyage from the roots of our mom's (Kukla's) and grandmother's (*yiayia's*) recipes to the family kitchen (*kouzina*) where history was reinvented.

One of the few unspoiled isles in the Aegean and a utopia of culinary delights, Karpathos—the second largest island of the Dodecanese chain, nestled between its more renowned neighbors Crete and Rhodes—is the ideal backdrop for *Kukla's Kouzina: A Gourmet Journey~Greek Island Style*, a series of cookbooks that contains a collection of recipes enriched by a woman with vision, transporting conventional foods to a level of unparalleled excellence. Awe-inspiring as the Titans, the elder gods who made Karpathos their home, this anthology will give you a rare glimpse into the flavors that ascend as high as their mythological ancestors. It's a slice of heaven about which the myths only hint! Extracted from the unspoiled mountain village of Olympos/Olymbos, which remains frozen in time, to the inland farming town of Volada, to the age-old fishing port of Finiki, these recipes remain true to their heritage with an originality that sets them apart from standard Greek cuisine—this is an edible trip worth tasting!

To become truly familiar with a culture one must live with its natives, breathe the same air, and of course, sample its foods. Foods reveal a story of the people who create them—cultures of the sea have diets abundant in fish, those inland take from the earth, and their mutual use of spices reflects the passion they happily share. On Karpathos, all of these elements combine to tell the tale of a civilization with a generous lifestyle that makes holidays and *every* day a celebration.

One memorable summer, we experienced that celebratory lifestyle firsthand while vacationing in Karpathos with our mom. We learned that weddings are a particularly festive island event where everyone is invited, including visitors, to partake not only in the couple's joy but also in the food event to follow, seating up to nine hundred people in barnlike structures. Friends and family join in to prepare the feast; caterers are replaced by cousins in aprons; and it's no surprise to find Uncle Demetri pouring the wine! Lemon-oregano marinated lamb is roasted outdoors on a spit, trays of vegetable-laden *moussaka* and béchamel-layered *pastitsio* are passed around, and delicate heart-shaped powdered-sugar-coated shortbread cookies, *kourambiedes*, are shared and devoured. Once the indigenous hospitality of Karpathos has touched your heart and ignited your appetite, you can't help but want to take it home and create it in your own kitchen. This cookbook series of our mom's perfected recipes will allow you to do just that.

Kukla's Kouzina: A Gourmet Journey~Greek Island Style is the first recipe collection ever released that is solely dedicated to this Greek island's culinary fare, an overlooked food genre until now. This is an in-depth opportunity for you to explore uncharted territory in an exceptional category.

The old adage about variety being the spice of life holds true. And life is even spicier when you home in on a society imbued with a particularly captivating gastronomy that has yet to be unveiled.

IT'S ALL GREEK TO ME...AND *YOU!* WHY?

Greek cuisine is one of today's most popular dining options. Why? It's simple...or complex—that's what Greek cooking is all about, literally! Whether easy as a peasant dish or involved as royal pastry (or anything in between), it's this range of foods that excites the palate and keeps Greek cuisine lovers in love!

A DISH BY ANY OTHER NAME

The differences between Karpathian cooking and mainstream Greek cuisine are apparent in a number of dishes that share a common name but actually have their own distinct food personalities, especially since our Kukla put her artistically dramatic signature on them. Everything had to look as good as it tasted, which was a challenge in and of itself—and Mom loved a good challenge. In fact, she thrived on it! The following examples are proof positive that a rose, or dish, by any other name is just as sweet...or savory.

Tyropitakia me Spitiko Fillo (Mini Cheese Pies with Homemade Dough) are not only scrumptious, but stunning when the edges are adorned with a twist decoration and sprinkled with sesame, as they are in Karpathos. *(Recipe on page 26, Pastries chapter.)*

Savory *spanakopites Karpathikes* (Karpathian spinach pies) do not mimic the well-known *spanakopita* but exhibit their own distinctive, undeniable charm. Spice-scented homemade dough half-moons from our *yiayia's* recipe collection are filled with a spinach and rice mixture that is lightly flavored with herbs. These individual pies are baked until risen, golden, and aromatic. A companion to this island recipe is our mom's phyllo *spanakopita* made with feta cheese, which is puffed like a soufflé when baked instead of being flat and dense like the traditional version.

In the world of everyday pasta dishes, most think of a tomato-based sauce. In Karpathos, pasta takes on a whole new meaning. *Makarounes,* an island specialty, is a peasant dish made up of homemade finger-rolled pasta (like cavatelli), onion, olive oil, and grated cheese. Although this sounds too simple to fall into the

A typical Olympos eatery where the dishes feature ingredients like lamb and squash blossoms (right).
The local tradition is to bake the food-laden trays in a rustic, wood-burning oven (left, rear).

realm of Greek cuisine, one forkful will prove that you don't need a dozen ingredients and hours slaving over a hot stove to make a delicious Karpathian dish. Quick, easy, and entirely satisfying!

Roasted lamb goes underground in *arnaki kleftiko* (slow-baked spring lamb)**.** In Greek, *arnaki* is *baby lamb* and *kleftiko* means *stolen.* In Karpathian history, thieves (*kleftes*) lived hidden in the mountains and would steal a lamb or goat and slow-cook the meat (up to twenty-four hours) in the ground in a sealed pit so there would be no smell, no visible smoke, and no sign of a stolen animal. The meat was so tender and delicious that the recipe was passed down through the generations and was named after the thieves. In Karpathos, *kleftiko* is still made the old-fashioned way (isn't that usually the best?), on the bone, marinated in garlic and lemon juice, and slow-baked in a pit-oven. Sometimes it's wrapped in parchment and baked in a clay pot.

Unlike mainland baklava, *Karpathikos mbaklavas* (Karpathian baklava) is made with an olive oil-based pastry dough that is rolled into a spiral, then sliced and deep-fried. Once drained and cooled, the diamond-shaped, flaky slices are drenched in a fragrant, spiced honey syrup and sprinkled with walnuts. The challenging accomplishment for our mom was getting the dough consistency just right to create a light, crisp pastry. Made for special celebrations, these extraordinary treats are piled high on trays, wrapped in colorful cellophane, and tied with elaborate bows. Our mom's decorations were as ornate and eye-catching as the pastries themselves!

(Recipes for the above will be included in our upcoming cookbooks.)

The *kellos* (the room used as a kitchen) in the Karpathian House—complete with a fireplace and *anakapnea* (chimney)—is where the stovetop cooking happens (think *avgolemono* soup, *stifado*, and *dolmades*). This is the core of daily family life, as it is in most modern homes...hey, we all love to eat, and there's no better place to be to steal a taste before dinner! An outdoor oven keeps the heat out of the main house in the hot summer months, and it's also used by neighboring families. This is where the breads, lamb, and *spanakopites* are made.

Other indigenous foods found on the island include full-cream cheeses like salty *almotyri/armotyri* and spiced *meriari* served with a variety of rustic bread loaves and *kouloures* (doughnut-shaped breads and biscuits made with wheat, barley, or a combination of both), *psilokouloura* (thin, sesame-covered, olive-oil breadsticks), *kouloumbotes* olives, *ofto* (baked lamb or goat stuffed with rice), *skaros yahni* (baked fish or "Karpathian fish" as the locals call it because the *skaros* fish can only be found in the Karpathian sea), *kavourmas/kavroumas* (strips of pork, similar to bacon, that are fried and served with bread), *lahanopita* (cabbage pie), *drilla* (a thick goat's-milk sour cream), *vyzanti* (lamb stuffed with bulgur or rice and baked in a wood-burning oven), and *hondros* (meat prepared with bulgur).

Fishing boat in Pigadia (left). Olympos ladies in customary dress. The *mantili/mandili* (μαντήλι, handkerchief head wrap) is worn on the island to protect their hair from the brisk daily breezes.

Pastries are also abundant and include *xylikopites* (pies made with creamed cheese, honey, and sugar), sweet *tourtes* or *sitakopita/myzithropita* (mini pies or tray-size pies prepared with locally-made sheep's- and/or goat's-milk *sitaka* or *myzithra* cheeses), *alevria* cookies (the dough kneaded in honey and butter), *sousamomelo/sisamomelo* (a sesame-and-honey confection served at weddings), and *poungia* (a Carnival cheese crescent with spices and honey).

KARPATHIAN HISTORY

The history of Karpathos tells the story of pieces of a puzzle that, over centuries, came together to form what is now known as Karpathian cuisine. These are the roots of one woman's culinary vision, a woman who refined this rich style of cookery! *Kukla's Kouzina: A Gourmet Journey~Greek Island Style* gives an in-depth perusal into this treasure trove of regional island cuisine and culture, taking Greek cooking to enchanting new heights. Our Kukla's customization of these foods makes them first-time originals.

This *Meze* cookbook features over twenty recipes, from our complete 150-recipe cookbook, that explore the diversity of flavors and culture from the remote villages in the north to the southernmost Dodecanese islands of Greece. This diversity has brought subtle (and sometimes not so subtle) nuances to this Mediterranean fare—making each island unique in its meals and customs. This diversity is an effect of not only climate and location, but also of occupation by various civilizations recurring throughout history as a result of wars and invasions. Karpathian history dates as far back as 2500 B.C.

Records show that the island was inhabited by numerous outside cultures, beginning in Neolithic times with the Minoans, who introduced a variety of foods from the sea, as well as savory olives and their complex flavorful oils, herbs such as oregano, and thyme-scented honey. The Minoans were followed by the Mycenaeans, whose culture was rich in farm-fresh (as well as dried) fruits and vegetables, sheep and goat dairy products, game meats, chicken, celery, cardamom, mint, and fennel. Then the Phoenicians transported wine to the island's shores. The Dorians came next with their Spartan diet of olive oil, garlic, pomegranates, figs, whole grains, apples, grapes, flax seeds, lentils, and a number of other high-nutrient staples we now refer to as superfoods. The Romans arrived with barley, millet, wheat, and cheese, all of which were infused with honey in certain recipes. The Venetians added pasta to the Karpathian diet, which led to the creation of *pastitsio*. And the language of the Ottomans inspired recipe names such as *moussaka*, *tzatziki*, *giouvarlakia*, *keftedes*, and *mboureki*. There was even a Genovese basil-loving pirate, Moresco, who ruled over the island. Aromas of citrus, allspice, cinnamon, and *vanilia* (pure vanillin or crystalline vanilla) dominate Karpathian cooking, and it is unknown whether they sprouted here and were taught to others or vice versa. Tomatoes became incorporated into Greek cuisine in the late nineteenth century and were widely used in Dodecanese cooking during the Italian occupation from 1912 to 1947.

Food in Karpathos is prepared using homegrown ingredients. It's been that way for centuries because, as an isolated island, it's difficult to get supplies from the mainland. There are also very few markets on the island, so when ingredients are needed, the natives go to the source.

Thyme honey comes from their bee farms and is extracted from their own honeycombs. Fruit and vegetables are grown organically. Cheese is made from the milk of their sheep and goats. Bread is baked using their own grains that are ground in their gristmills powered by the wind. If you're eating in Karpathos, most of the ingredients are as local as local gets. This is the purest form of the farm-to-table movement.

These influences, combined with the island's faithful native roots, have made Karpathos incomparable in its novel style and preparation of food, creating a culinary icon that lives only on this distinct island and is enhanced in the pages of this book.

Now step into our *kouzina* and learn firsthand about what makes our cuisine so different from the other corners of Greece, and what makes it so irresistible.

Kali orexi!

Καλή όρεξη!

Good appetite!

PREPARATION

GO GREEK COOKING 101...*THE BASICS!*

Get ready to have all of your inhibitions about cooking Greek stripped away. Between our *Kukla's Kouzina: A Gourmet Journey~Greek Island Style* cookbook series and our blog (at *kuklaskouzina.com*), we'll help you avoid the pitfalls of things like working with cracking phyllo dough, and dealing with lumps in the béchamel sauce in recipes like *Mbourekia me Tyri* (Cheese Rolls), page 28. Our step-by-step instructions and online how-to videos will walk you through the Greek cooking process, simplifying your experience. Techniques on how to work with phyllo, how to make *Dolmadakia* and Greek yogurt, and more can be found in our *Greek Cooking Techniques* chapter, page 43. Unique ingredients used in Greek cooking and baking are listed and defined in *Kouzina A to Ω:* Ingredients, page 48, with shopping options offered in *Greek Food & Product Sources*, page 62.

Greek cooking not only *can* be complicated but *is* complicated at times, so preparation will be your key to success! Get organized and plan ahead. To help you budget your time, our recipes list preparation and cooking/baking times, along with their degree of difficulty (from easy to challenging), and number of servings. Use common sense. If you know you're slower or more meticulous in the kitchen (*which is totally okay!*), give yourself some extra time. Don't make something involved like pastries or bread on a day you have concert tickets.

Read through the recipe a couple of times to get familiar with the ingredients and which ones you'll need to put on your shopping list, the cookware and utensils that are used, and how much time it'll take for preparation and cooking/baking. Is there anything in the recipe that needs to be done beforehand, like defrosting phyllo? Are there any ingredients that can be prepared a few hours ahead or a day or two in advance, like grating cheese? Getting a head start will save you time in the kitchen when you're assembling your recipe. You'll be surprised at how easy Greek cooking (or any kind of cooking) can be when you take a few minutes to familiarize yourself with the dish you choose to make.

Recipes list ingredients in the order they're used, so after you measure, chop, weigh, etc., line everything up on your workspace in the order listed. Do the same with your measuring spoons/cups, cooking utensils, and cookware. If you're baking or roasting (not broiling), preheat the oven to the temperature listed for at least 15 minutes before using. Prepare your baking pans/sheets (grease and/or flour, if instructed) before starting.

Kukla made it a practice to clean as she went. This practice keeps your workspace (and your mind) tidy. Start by making sure your sink and dishwasher have been emptied so you'll have room for your dirty bowls, pans, etc. Better yet, draft one (or more) of your kids to be your sous-chef (deputy cook). Get them a chef's hat or a special apron with their name on it so they feel they're an important part of your kitchen team. Let them help you measure out ingredients and ask them to clean up behind you (a.k.a. wash dishes or fill the dishwasher). Spills happen, so have a sponge or paper towels handy to wipe them up right away. Keeping it clean will help you to remain organized, work faster, and stay focused.

If you're making something like *Tyropitakia Trigona me Fillo* (Phyllo Cheese Triangles), page 30, or *Dolmadakia me Klimatofilla* (Stuffed Grape Leaves), page 40, draft your sous-chef to help you fill, fold, and roll. Your kids will love it, plus it'll cut your prep time in half and you'll have company to make it fun!

Enjoy each step of the Greek cooking and baking process...maybe put on some Greek music to get you in that Mediterranean mood. We recommend *Stamatis Kokotas Unforgettable Hits* for classic Greek, or for today's sound try chart-topper Giannis Ploutarhos—he's the hottest thing going.

Make cooking special by bringing your family to the preparation table as well as the dining table...you'll reap the delicious rewards when you sit down to eat. The family that cooks Greek together says *"OPA!"* together...but use the dishes for serving, not for breaking (they play it up in the movies, but *we don't really do that at home*)!

MEZE

APPETIZERS & PETITE PLATES

The tempting first offerings that can make or break a dinner party should tease the palate and hint at the delectable things to come. They should be tantalizing, inviting, and flirtatious, but never filling. That pleasure is to be satisfied gradually by the courses to follow. Learning how to arrange appetizers and knowing which will pair well together is as key as the appetizers themselves. Kukla's how-to tips and our photos help to demonstrate the power of mixing and matching. Preparation and cooking times help you plan your time in the kitchen, and the degree of difficulty is listed so you'll know if a particular recipe is something you can handle. Whether "easy" is your speed or you never back away from a "challenging" recipe, we'll take you through the process so you can enjoy it and reap the tasty rewards. Whenever possible, substitutions are offered, and following the recipes you'll find the chapters *Greek Cooking Techniques*, *Kouzina A to Ω: Equipment, Ingredients, Common Cooking Methods & Food Terms of Greek Island Cuisine*, and *Greek Food & Product Sources* (in-store and online) to help make your experience full and fun.

In the Greek home, wine and spirits are a natural part of the eating experience, so following the chapter descriptions below, you'll find suggestions for Greek libations that will best match the recipes within each section (Greek coffee also goes well with *mezedes*). Specific wine- and spirit-pairings can be found on our website's blog.

SPREADS & DIPS

Whether served as an appetizer (*orektiko*, ορεκτικό) or as an accompaniment to a main course, the delicious recipes in this chapter are essential elements of the Greek island table. A colorful assortment of spreads and dips—golden *Houmous* (Hummus), black *Pasta Elias* (Olive Paste/Spread), white *Tzatziki* (Yogurt-Cucumber Sauce/Dip), coral *Taramosalata* (Carp Roe Spread), ivory *Skordalia* (Garlic Sauce/Dip), and sage-green *Melitzanosalata* (Eggplant-Salad Spread), sectioned off by cucumber slices and interspersed with deep-purple kalamata olives—make a powerful statement when arranged side-by-side on a large platter, drawing the eye and whetting the palate. Or let art be your guide and arrange them in individual bowls to create a painter's palate (as we did on page 14). A basket of grilled pita wedges on the side completes the picture.

Wine Pairing: Semi-dry white or dry rosé

PASTRIES

Savory mini pastries wrapped in homemade dough and phyllo dominate this chapter, and will add a delightful dimension to your meze table. From bite-size *Spanaki* and *Elia Sfoliata* (Spinach and Olive Puffs) to palm-size *Tyropitakia* (Cheese Pies) and *Mbourekia* (Cheese and Meat Rolls), these pastries can be served alongside our spreads and dips to enhance your menu, and will also stand alone nicely at a cocktail party. Always use imported Greek or Bulgarian sheep's-milk feta for the most authentic and delicious results.

Wine Pairing: Red varietal / *Spirit Pairing:* Greek brandy (such as Metaxa), Ouzo, or Tsipouro

PETITE PLATES

For a substantial meze presentation, the recipes in this chapter will not only add that hearty element, but will be the perfect prelude to a light meal. These versatile foods are also ideal for a sampler dinner made up of a variety of small or "petite" plates. The mini-course tasting will delight your guests and make your party eclectic and festive. *Saganaki* (Fried Greek Cheese Flambé) straight from the frying pan has a tangy citrus finish. Pineapple shell-plated shrimp gets a boost from Kukla's and our Uncle Bill's piquant sauce in *Garides me Saltsa Kokteil* (Greek Shrimp Cocktail). Mushroom caps are filled with *kefalograviera* cheese and walnuts in *Gemista Manitaria* (Stuffed Mushrooms). The centers of cone-shaped ham slices are piped with an egg-and-pickle mixture in *Kanape me Zampon* (Ham Canapés). The cool *Tzatziki* (Yogurt-Cucumber Sauce/Dip), from *Spreads & Dips*, nicely complements herbed *Keftedakia* (Cocktail Meatballs), while warm *Avgolemono* pairs well with zesty *Dolmadakia* (Stuffed Grape Leaves). Individually or in any combination, these petite plates will fill your rich meze table with grandeur!

Wine Pairing: Semi-dry red, white, or rosé / *Spirit Pairing:* Greek brandy (such as Metaxa), Ouzo, or Tsipouro

Spreads & Dips

Clockwise from top left:
Carp (fish) Roe Spread,
Eggplant-Salad Spread, Garlic
Sauce/Dip, Olive Paste/Spread,
Lemon-Pepper Hummus

Lemon-Pepper Hummus

χούμους με λεμόνι και πιπέρι
HOUMOUS ME LEMONI KAI PIPERI

One recipe, four ways—each flavor variation below can be mixed into the hummus or served as a dollop in the center. For a party, try making all of these varieties and place them side by side on a serving tray for a colorful, appetizing presentation.
Pictured on opposite page.

1 can (20 ounces) chickpeas, rinsed
    and drained
½ cup fresh lemon juice (about
    3 lemons)
3 tablespoons extra-virgin olive oil
1 tablespoon tahini
1 small garlic clove, minced
½ teaspoon fine sea salt
⅛ teaspoon freshly ground pepper

Diced orange bell pepper, for
    garnish
Pita bread wedges, crackers, or
    vegetables (cucumber slices,
    baby carrots, bell pepper slices,
    celery), for serving

TOTAL PREP TIME 10 minutes plus chilling
DIFFICULTY LEVEL easy
MAKES about 2 cups, serving 6 to 8

In a food processor, combine all of the ingredients and process until smooth, about 1 minute. *(Can be made ahead. Transfer to an airtight container and refrigerate up to 3 days.)* Transfer to a serving bowl and garnish the center of the *houmous* with diced bell pepper, if desired. Serve slightly chilled (refrigerate 1 hour) or at room temperature with pita, crackers, or vegetables on the side.

VARIATIONS:
Sun-dried Tomato Hummus
χούμους με λιαστή ντομάτα
HOUMOUS ME LIASTI NTOMATA
Substitute *¼ cup vegetable broth* for half of the lemon juice. In a food processor, process *¼ cup drained julienned sun-dried tomatoes* (from a jar, packed in olive oil) and *4 large fresh basil leaves (or ¼ teaspoon dried)* until finely chopped, then add the remaining *houmous* ingredients and process until smooth, or spoon the sun-dried tomato mixture into the center of the chilled *houmous* and serve.

Olive Hummus
χούμους με ελιές
HOUMOUS ME ELIES
In a food processor, process *¼ cup pitted kalamata olives* (adding more or less, to taste) until finely chopped, then add the remaining *houmous* ingredients and process until smooth, or spoon the chopped olives into the center of the chilled *houmous* and serve.

Artichoke and Spinach Hummus
χούμους με αγκινάρες και σπανάκι
HOUMOUS ME AGINARES KAI SPANAKI
In a food processor, process *¼ cup thawed frozen artichoke hearts* and *¼ cup fresh spinach leaves* until chopped, then add the remaining *houmous* ingredients and process until smooth, or spoon the artichoke-spinach mixture into the center of the chilled *houmous* and serve.

Olive Paste/Spread

πάστα ελιάς

PASTA ELIAS

Here's an easy and inexpensive way to make and enjoy this classic Greek condiment that's bursting with fresh flavor. Fast and delicious, what could be better?
Pictured on page 14.

8 ounces pitted kalamata or green Greek olives, or a combination of both
2 tablespoons extra-virgin olive oil
⅛ teaspoon minced garlic (1 small clove)
1 teaspoon fresh oregano leaves or ¼ teaspoon dried

Fresh oregano sprigs and thinly sliced lemon zest, for garnish
Pita bread wedges or crackers, for serving

TOTAL PREP TIME 10 minutes plus standing and chilling
DIFFICULTY LEVEL easy
MAKES 1 cup, serving 4 to 6

1. Check the olives to make sure there are no pits or pit fragments, then place them in a large bowl and add enough cold water to cover by 2 inches. Let stand, changing water occasionally, until most of the salt is removed, 2 to 3 hours. Keep in mind that not all olives are created equally and some are saltier than others. They should be a little salty after soaking, so taste to see if they're ready. After soaking, drain the olives well, squeezing out any excess water, then pat dry with paper towels.

2. Transfer the olives to a food processor and pulse until very finely chopped or pureed, about 15 seconds. With the motor running, gradually pour in the oil through the feed tube. Add the garlic and oregano and process until combined well. Transfer the *pasta elias* to a serving bowl, cover, and refrigerate at least 1 hour before serving to thicken. *(Can be made ahead. Transfer to an airtight container and refrigerate up to 3 days.)*

3. *To serve:* Garnish the *pasta elias* with oregano sprigs and lemon zest, if desired. Serve slightly chilled (refrigerate 1 hour) or at room temperature with pita or crackers on the side.

Yogurt-Cucumber Sauce/Dip

τζατζίκι
TZATZIKI

Served as a dipping sauce with pita bread or as an accompaniment to our herbed mini Cocktail Meatballs (*Keftedakia*, page 39), gyro, souvlaki, roast lamb, or vegetable dishes, *Tzatziki* is a staple in Greek cooking—and our version has the ideal balance of flavor and thickness. *Pictured with Cocktail Meatballs on page 38.*

1 medium cucumber (¾ pound),
   peeled and cut in half lengthwise
¼ cup extra-virgin olive oil
2 garlic cloves, minced or 1 teaspoon
   garlic powder
½ teaspoon fine sea salt
¼ teaspoon freshly ground pepper
16 ounces thick Greek yogurt or
   Drained Yogurt (recipe below)
3 tablespoons whole milk
1½ tablespoons chopped fresh dill,
   plus sprigs for garnish

Pita bread wedges, chips, or
   vegetable sticks, for serving

TOTAL PREP TIME 15 minutes plus chilling
DIFFICULTY LEVEL easy
MAKES 2 ¼ cups, serving 8 to 10

1. Using a spoon, scoop out the seeds from the cucumber (discard seeds) and coarsely grate over a medium bowl (you should have 1 cup grated cucumber). Add the oil, garlic, salt, and pepper, and stir until combined. Stir in the yogurt until combined well. Add the milk and stir until smooth, then stir in the dill. Transfer the *tzatziki* to a serving bowl, cover, and refrigerate at least 30 minutes or overnight. (*Can be made ahead. Transfer to an airtight container and refrigerate up to 2 days. When ready to serve, stir to incorporate any water that separates out of the* tzatziki.)

2. *To serve:* Garnish the *tzatziki* with dill sprigs, if desired. Serve chilled with pita, chips, or vegetable sticks on the side.

DRAINED YOGURT

When yogurt is called for in Greek cooking, it is drained (strained) Greek sheep's-milk yogurt, which is the consistency of cream cheese. Sheep's-milk yogurt is sweeter and creamier than cow's-milk and is available in Greek markets and gourmet shops. You can also use thick Mediterranean-style sheep's-milk or cow's-milk yogurt, available in supermarkets and specialty food stores throughout the United States. Our homemade drained yogurt is an acceptable substitute.

32 ounces (4 cups) plain (unflavored) whole-milk yogurt

Line a fine mesh sieve with a double thickness of cheesecloth and place it over a large bowl. Place the yogurt in the cheesecloth, gather up the sides, and tie them together with kitchen twine. Cover the bowl with plastic wrap and let the yogurt drain in the refrigerator until very thick, 2 to 4 hours or overnight (discard the water that collects in the bowl). Makes 16 ounces (2 cups) Drained Yogurt.

Garlic Sauce/Dip

σκορδαλιά

SKORDALIA

This well-known Greek sauce can vary from mild (featured here) to intense in flavor (the way Kukla made it, with an entire head of garlic). Feel free to adjust the amount of garlic to your taste. Kukla used a mortar (*goudi*) and pestle to mash the garlic but along came the food processor, taking the muscle out of the prep. Serve as a meze with pita bread, over boiled, grilled, or fried vegetables, or alongside fish.
Pictured on page 14.

1 pound russet or Yukon Gold
   potatoes, peeled and cut into
   1-inch cubes
1 slice firm white bread, crust
   removed
½ cup extra-virgin olive oil, divided
1 ½ teaspoons minced garlic (about
   3 cloves) or more, to taste
5 tablespoons fresh lemon juice
   (from 2 lemons)
2 ½ tablespoons white vinegar
½ teaspoon fine sea salt

Thinly sliced shallot or red onion,
   for garnish
Pita bread wedges or vegetable
   sticks, for serving

PREP TIME 15 minutes
COOKING TIME 20 minutes
DIFFICULTY LEVEL easy
MAKES about 2 cups, serving 8 to 10

1. In a large saucepan, bring the potatoes with enough cold water to cover by 2 inches to a boil over medium-high heat. Reduce the heat to a low boil and cook until the potatoes are fork-tender but not falling apart, about 15 minutes. Drain well, then press through a ricer into a large bowl.

2. Meanwhile, place the bread in a shallow bowl, cover with cold water, and let stand until just soaked through, about 1 minute. Squeeze the water out of the bread (discard the water) and transfer the bread to a food processor. Pulse 2 to 3 times, until the bread is the consistency of fine crumbs. Add ¼ cup oil and the garlic, and pulse until smooth, about 10 seconds. Add the lemon juice, vinegar, salt, and the remaining ¼ cup oil. Pulse until smooth, about 15 seconds. Add the potato to the processor and pulse, stirring occasionally and scraping down the sides with a spatula, until smooth, about 1 minute (do not over process as this can make the *skordalia* pasty). Transfer the *skordalia* to a serving bowl. *(Can be made ahead. Transfer to an airtight container and refrigerate up to 3 days.)*

3. *To serve:* Garnish the *skordalia* with shallot or red onion slices, if desired. Serve at room temperature with pita or vegetable sticks on the side.

Carp (fish) Roe Spread

ταραμοσαλάτα

TARAMOSALATA

Tarama (carp or cod roe), the main ingredient in this spread, is considered the *Greek* caviar. This relatively inexpensive roe is aged and cured for over a year and is extremely salty, making the addition of salt in recipes in which *tarama* is used unnecessary. *Taramosalata* is appropriate for fasting periods and is a valued food during Lent, though it's delicious enough to be savored anytime.
Pictured on page 14.

10 ounces russet potatoes, peeled and cut into 1-inch cubes
1 cup extra-virgin olive oil
½ cup fresh lemon juice (about 3 lemons)
1 teaspoon finely minced shallot
½ cup *tarama* (carp roe)
2 tablespoons lemon seltzer or carbonated water

Capers, parsley sprigs, and/or olives, for garnish
Pita bread wedges or crackers, for serving

PREP TIME 20 minutes plus chilling
COOKING TIME 20 minutes
DIFFICULTY LEVEL easy
MAKES 2 ¼ cups, serving 8 to 10

1. In a 2-quart saucepan, bring the potatoes with enough cold water to cover by 2 inches to a boil over medium-high heat. Reduce the heat to a low boil and cook until the potatoes are fork-tender but not falling apart, about 15 minutes. Drain well, then press through a ricer into a mixer bowl.

2. Beat the potato on medium speed while alternately, and very gradually, pouring in the oil and lemon juice, beating well after each addition, until the oil is absorbed and the mixture is creamy, light, and fluffy, about 5 minutes. Add the shallot and beat until combined well, about 30 seconds. Beat in the *tarama* until combined well, about 20 seconds. Beat in the seltzer just until combined. Transfer the *taramosalata* to a serving bowl, cover tightly, and refrigerate at least 1 hour or overnight. *(Can be made ahead. Transfer to an airtight container and refrigerate up to 4 days. The flavor is best after 1 to 2 days.)*

3. *To serve:* Garnish the *taramosalata* with capers, parsley, and/or olives, if desired. Serve chilled with pita or crackers on the side.

THEN AND NOW

Kukla used to grind the roe in an old wooden mortar (*goudi*) and pestle. This broke down the roe so the flavor could easily blend with the other ingredients. She then whisked the roe into an emulsion with olive oil and lemon juice, followed by beating in potato to thicken it. Here, we all worked together to simplify her method and make the prep quick and easy, while ensuring that it's just as delicious. The result is a fluffy, mousse-like, vibrant coral-colored spread.

KOUZINA TIP—COLOR CUE

The color of this delicious spread, which can range from a warm beige to coral to a pink, comes from the type or brand of roe used. Roe colors range from orange carp (featured in this recipe) to pale-pink cod to red lumpfish and will result in a coral-, buff/blush-, or pink-colored spread, respectively. Olive oil is also a factor. When dark in color, olive oil can turn the spread beige, regardless of the color of the roe. If you'd like to avoid this, choose an olive oil that is light in color so the spread will more closely reflect the color of the roe. Let the roe and olive-oil pigments guide you. The type of potato used is another color factor. Because potato is the base for this spread, we use russet potatoes to keep the color neutral so the vibrant roe can shine through. For a subtle natural rose hue, try adding a touch of beet juice (1 teaspoon to 1 tablespoon).

Eggplant-Salad Spread

μελιτζανοσαλάτα
MELITZANOSALATA

This fresh and delicious spread can be made with or without tomato—both versions are amazing. For a stunning presentation, serve this spread as part of a *pikilia* (variety) platter with Carp Roe Spread, Garlic Sauce/Dip, Olive Paste/Spread, Lemon-Pepper Hummus, and Yogurt-Cucumber Sauce/Dip (*as pictured on page* 14), or plate side-by-side, each spread/dip separated by thin slices of cucumber and apple.

2 pounds eggplant (about 2 large eggplants)
⅓ cup extra-virgin olive oil, divided
¼ cup chopped scallion (about 2 scallions)
2 garlic cloves, minced
¼ cup packed fresh flat-leaf parsley leaves, plus sprigs for garnish
2 tablespoons capers, rinsed and drained
2 tablespoons red wine vinegar
½ teaspoon fine sea salt
¼ teaspoon freshly ground pepper
1 large firm, ripe beefsteak tomato (about 1 pound), cored, peeled, seeded, finely chopped, and drained, plus more for garnish, optional

Pita bread wedges or sliced French bread, for serving

PREP TIME 30 minutes
COOKING TIME 4 minutes
BROILING / GRILLING TIME 25 minutes
DIFFICULTY LEVEL easy
MAKES 3 cups with tomato / 2 ¼ cups without tomato, serving 6 to 8

1. Arrange a rack 6 inches from the broiler element and preheat the broiler. Wash the eggplants and pat dry with paper towels, then lightly coat them with oil. Place the whole eggplants on a heavy-duty rimmed baking sheet and broil, turning every few minutes, until the skins are charred on all sides and the flesh softens, about 20 minutes (you can also do this on a grill set at medium heat). Transfer the eggplants on the sheet to a wire rack and let them stand until cool enough to handle but still very warm (this will make peeling them easier).

2. Meanwhile, in a small skillet, heat 2 tablespoons oil over medium heat. Add the scallion and sauté, stirring occasionally, until just golden, about 2 minutes. Add the garlic and cook until aromatic, about 1 minute more. Transfer to a large heatproof bowl and set aside.

3. Peel the eggplants and cut each in half lengthwise, reserving any liquid in a bowl. Remove and discard as many seeds as possible and cut the flesh into 1-inch chunks. Broil the eggplant chunks on the same baking sheet (or grill) for about 5 minutes more, until the edges are browned and the eggplant is cooked through and fork-tender. Transfer the eggplant to a food processor along with the reserved eggplant liquid, the parsley, capers, vinegar, salt, pepper, and the remaining oil. Process until slightly chunky or almost smooth, as desired. Transfer to the bowl with the scallion mixture and stir to combine, then stir in the tomato (if using). Transfer the *melitzanosalata* to a serving bowl and serve at room temperature or chilled (for chilled, cover and refrigerate at least 2 hours or overnight). *(Can be made ahead. Transfer to an airtight container and refrigerate up to 2 days.)*

4. *To serve:* Garnish the *melitzanosalata* with chopped tomato and parsley sprigs, if desired. Serve at room temperature or chilled with pita or French bread on the side.

Pastries

Spinach Puffs

σπανάκι σφολιάτα
SPANAKI SFOLIATA

These flaky mini-puffs resemble spinach pie and are an exquisitely scrumptious meze.
To simplify your party menu, the puffs can be made ahead and be refrigerated or
frozen, then reheated in just 10 minutes.

KUKLA'S PAIRING Serve with champagne or wine.

DOUGH
2 ¼ cups all-purpose flour, plus
    more for kneading and rolling
2 ¼ teaspoons baking powder
¼ plus ⅛ teaspoon nutmeg
Pinch *vanilia*/vanillin (powdered
    crystalline vanilla)*
Fine sea salt
6 tablespoons butter, softened
2 ¼ teaspoons vegetable
    shortening
1 ½ tablespoons Greek brandy/
    cognac (like Metaxa)
3 large eggs, separated
6 tablespoons thick Greek yogurt
6 tablespoons freshly grated
    kefalograviera cheese (or
    Parmigiano-Reggiano)
6 tablespoons freshly grated dry
    myzithra cheese (or dry-aged
    ricotta salata)

FILLING
1 tablespoon extra-virgin olive oil
½ cup chopped onion (about
    1 small onion)
¼ cup thinly sliced scallion (about
    2 scallions)
5 ounces fresh spinach leaves,
    washed, drained well, and
    chopped into ½-inch pieces
3 tablespoons chopped fresh flat-
    leaf parsley
2 tablespoons chopped fresh dill
½ teaspoon powdered chicken
    bouillon
⅔ cup crumbled feta cheese (about
    3 ounces)
1 ¾ ounces breakfast-sausage links
    (about 1 ½ links), fried until crisp,
    cooled, finely chopped (¼ cup)

PREP TIME 2 ¼ hours plus standing
COOKING TIME 15 minutes
BAKING TIME 50 minutes
DIFFICULTY LEVEL moderate
MAKES 21 spinach puffs

1. *Make dough:* In a large bowl, sift together the flour, baking powder, nutmeg, *vanilia*, and ⅛ teaspoon salt. Set aside.

2. In a large mixer bowl, beat together the butter and vegetable shortening on medium speed until light and fluffy, about 3 minutes. Reduce speed to low and beat in the brandy until combined well, about 1 minute. Add the egg yolks, one at a time, beating well after each addition. Add the yogurt and beat until combined, about 2 minutes; set aside. In a clean mixer bowl with clean beaters, beat the egg whites with a pinch of salt to stiff peaks. Fold into the butter mixture just until combined. Add the flour mixture and combine with hands, then knead until a sticky dough is formed. Gradually add and knead in the cheeses until combined well. Continue to knead until a soft dough is formed that can be rolled into balls, gradually adding up to 1 ½ tablespoons of flour, if needed. Place the dough in a lightly greased bowl, cover with a clean kitchen towel, and let stand at room temperature for 30 minutes.

3. *Meanwhile, make filling:* Arrange a rack in the center of the oven and heat to 350°F. In a large skillet, heat the oil over medium heat. Add the onion and cook until softened, 8 to 10 minutes. Add the scallion and sauté until lightly golden, about 2 minutes. Stir in the spinach, parsley, and dill, and cook until just wilted, about 3 minutes (do not over cook). Remove from heat. Drain well in a fine sieve, firmly pressing out excess liquid. Transfer the spinach mixture to a large heatproof bowl and stir in the bouillon until dissolved. Let cool to lukewarm. Toss in the feta and sausage, then stir in the egg, heavy cream, bread crumbs, salt, and pepper until combined well. Makes 1 ½ cups of filling.

4. On a lightly floured surface, roll out the dough to ⅛-inch thickness and cut into 21 3-inch squares. In an ungreased nonstick 24-cup mini-muffin pan, mold 1 square into each cavity, letting the corners extend over the edges. Divide the filling (about 1 tablespoon each) among them. Working with 1 filled square at a time, dab the ends of the 4 corners with water and bring them together in the center, overlapping them slightly, and pinch to seal. Fill the empty pan cups halfway with water

1 large egg, lightly beaten
2 tablespoons heavy or whipping
  cream
2 teaspoons plain dry bread crumbs
Pinch fine sea salt
Smidgen freshly ground pepper

1 large egg, beaten well, for brushing

(this will protect your pan and add moisture to the puffs while baking). Lightly brush the tops of the pastry with the beaten egg and bake until golden, about 50 minutes. *(Can be made ahead. Cool completely, then transfer to an airtight container and refrigerate up to 24 hours or freeze up to 1 month. Reheat puffs, unthawed if frozen, on a baking sheet in a preheated 350°F oven for 10 to 15 minutes.)* Serve hot.

*See *Greek Food & Product Sources* chapter for *vanilia* purchase options. The flavor of *vanilia* is exceptional, but in a pinch, substitute ¼ teaspoon vanilla extract and beat in after the egg yolks in step 2.

TIME-SAVER OPTION It's worth the extra time to make this delicious dough but if you need a quick alternative, this filling also works well in prebaked mini phyllo shells (in the freezer section of the supermarket). One recipe will fill 18 shells. Spoon 1 rounded tablespoon of filling into each shell, place on an ungreased cookie sheet, and bake in a 350°F oven until lightly golden, 30 to 35 minutes.

Olive Puffs

ελιά σφολιάτα
ELIA SFOLIATA

Kukla's effortless homemade cheesy puff pastry wraps around olives for a Greek take on Pigs-in-a-Blanket. The result is anything but ordinary!

KUKLA'S PAIRING Serve with a classic brandy cocktail.

DOUGH
1 cup all-purpose flour
1 teaspoon baking powder
1 teaspoon paprika
¼ teaspoon fine sea salt
6 ounces kasseri cheese, grated
　(1 cup)
6 ounces sharp cheddar cheese,
　grated (1 cup)
½ cup butter, softened

24 to 26 jarred medium-size
　pimento-stuffed green olives,
　soaked in water for 1 hour,
　drained well
1 large egg, beaten well, for
　brushing
Black sesame (*mavrosousamo*), for
　garnish
Whole-grain mustard, for serving

PREP TIME 40 minutes plus standing and chilling
BAKING TIME 15 minutes
DIFFICULTY LEVEL easy
MAKES 24 to 26 olive puffs

1. *Make dough:* In a large bowl, sift together the flour, baking powder, paprika, and salt. In a medium bowl, using a fork, mash together the kasseri, cheddar, and butter until combined well. Add the cheese mixture to the flour mixture and combine with hands until a soft dough forms. Shape the dough into a ball, wrap well in plastic wrap, and refrigerate at least 1 hour or up to 2 days. (If chilling overnight or longer, before using, let the dough stand at room temperature just until it's soft enough to roll into balls, about 30 minutes.)

2. Arrange a rack in the center of the oven and heat to 400°F. Pat the olives dry with paper towels. Wrap about 1 tablespoon of dough around each olive and place them 1 inch apart on an ungreased large heavy-duty rimmed baking sheet. Lightly brush the tops of the pastry with the beaten egg. Immediately sprinkle with black sesame, if desired. Bake until puffed and golden, about 15 minutes. *(Can be made ahead. Cool completely, then transfer to an airtight container and refrigerate up to 24 hours. Reheat puffs on a baking sheet in a preheated 350°F oven for about 8 minutes.)* Serve warm with mustard on the side.

KOUZINA TIP

This dough can be made and kept refrigerated up to 2 days ahead. Before using, the dough will need about 30 minutes at room temperature to soften, so spend that time preparing your workspace.

Mini Cheese Pies with Homemade Dough

τυροπιτάκια με σπιτικό φύλλο
TYROPITAKIA ME SPITIKO FILLO

Homemade dough makes these cheesy appetizers incredibly scrumptious, as well as stunning when the edges are decorated. Perfect for dinner parties or special occasions, they can be made ahead and frozen up to one month. Just pop them in the oven 15 minutes before the festivities begin and you can spend more time with your guests. To create our decorative, traditional twisted edge, make an additional half recipe of dough and follow the method at the end of the recipe. *Also pictured on the cover.*

DOUGH
5 ½ cups all-purpose flour, divided, plus more for rolling
1 tablespoon plus 1 ½ teaspoons baking powder
1 teaspoon baking soda
1 cup butter, softened
1 cup plain reduced fat (2%) thick Greek yogurt
3 tablespoons vegetable shortening
6 large eggs, separated
½ cup shredded kasseri cheese (for a cheesier dough add 2 tablespoons more)
½ cup shredded *kefalotyri* cheese (for a cheesier dough add 2 tablespoons more)

FILLING
5 ounces feta cheese, crumbled (about 1 ¼ cups)
½ cup *myzithra*, ricotta, or creamy small-curd cottage cheese (about 4 ounces)
¼ cup grated kasseri cheese
¼ cup grated *kefalotyri* cheese
1 large egg, lightly beaten
1 large egg yolk
½ tablespoon butter, melted
1 teaspoon dry bread crumbs
⅛ teaspoon nutmeg

1 large egg, lightly beaten, for brushing
2 tablespoons toasted sesame seeds, optional

PREP TIME 1 ½ hours
BAKING TIME 25 to 28 minutes per batch
DIFFICULTY LEVEL moderate
MAKES 40 *tyropitakia*

1. *Make dough:* In a large bowl, sift together 5 cups flour, the baking powder, and baking soda. Set aside.

2. In a large mixer bowl, beat the butter on medium speed just until creamy. Add the yogurt and beat until combined. Add the vegetable shortening and beat until combined. Add the egg yolks, one at a time, beating well after each addition (the mixture will look like oatmeal). Reduce speed to medium-low. Gradually add 1 cup of the flour mixture and beat just until combined. In a clean mixer bowl with clean beaters, beat the egg whites to stiff peaks. Fold the beaten whites into the batter, then fold in the shredded cheeses. Mix in the remaining flour mixture by hand and knead to make a soft dough. If the dough is sticky, add just enough of the remaining ½ cup flour, a little at a time, to smooth the dough. Shape the dough into a ball, return to the bowl, cover with a clean kitchen towel, and set aside.

3. *Make filling:* In a medium bowl, mix together all of the filling ingredients. (*Can be made ahead. Transfer to an airtight container and refrigerate up to 24 hours or freeze up to 1 week. If frozen, thaw in the refrigerator overnight before using.*) Makes 1 ½ cups of filling.

4. Arrange a rack in the center of the oven and heat to 350°F. Lightly grease 4 large heavy-duty rimmed baking sheets. Roll the dough into 40 balls (about 1 ½ inches in diameter). On a lightly floured surface, working with 1 ball at a time, press each into a 4-inch round, ¼-inch thick. Place about 1 ¾ teaspoons of filling in the center, leaving a ½-inch border around the edge. Brush the edges of the round with water, then lift and fold one side of the round over the filling so that the edges meet, forming a half moon. Using your fingertips, firmly press the edges to seal. Then, using the tines of a fork, press down on the edges to lightly score and secure the seal. Trim any uneven edges with a pastry wheel. (*For a decorative twisted edge, continue with the method at the end of this recipe.*) Place the *tyropitakia*, 1 inch apart, on the prepared baking sheets. When each sheet is full, lightly brush the tops with egg, sprinkle with sesame (if using), and bake until a light golden brown (the bottoms should be lightly browned as well), 25 to 28 minutes. (*Can*

KOUZINA TIP

This versatile dough can also be made into breadsticks. Simply roll into several breadstick shapes, like twists, brush with egg, sprinkle with sesame seeds (if desired), and bake at 350°F until golden brown, 25 to 28 minutes.

To make a long stuffed baguette, roll the dough out into a rectangle (about ¼-inch thick), sprinkle with *cooked bacon bits or crumbled sausage (¼ to ½ cup)*, then roll up from the long side into a baguette, and pinch the seam and ends to seal. Place, seam side down, on a greased baking sheet; brush with egg, sprinkle with sesame seeds (if desired), and bake at 350°F until golden brown, about 30 minutes.

For a pinwheel design, cut the baguette into 1-inch-thick slices, place them flat on the prepared baking sheet, and bake as directed above, 20 to 25 minutes.

be made ahead. Cool completely, then seal in heavy-duty resealable plastic bags and refrigerate up to 24 hours or freeze up to 1 month. Reheat tyropitakia, *thawed if frozen, on baking sheets in a preheated 350°F oven until heated through, about 15 minutes.)* Serve hot.

FOR DECORATIVE EDGE
In Karpathos, making foods look beautiful is a longstanding tradition, one that Kukla incorporated into everything she did, especially when it came to dough-wrapped pitas and breads. But with beauty comes work and time, so set aside an extra hour to decorate the *tyropitakia* edges with these twists.

METHOD
Make an additional ½ recipe of the dough for the twisted edges and divide it into 40 balls. For each *tyropitaki*, halve each ball and roll out into 2 thin ropes (about ⅛-inch thick). Twirl the ropes together to form a 9-inch-long twist. Brush the round edge of the *tyropitaki* with water, then arrange the twist along the edge, leaving a ½-inch overhang of twist on each end. Tuck the ends underneath the straight side of the *tyropitaki* and pinch the ends to secure. Lightly press down the twist to adhere around the edge. Continue with step 4 in the recipe, baking the decorated *tyropitakia* until a light golden brown, 30 to 35 minutes. For variety, after brushing with egg, sprinkle some *tyropitakia* with sesame just in the center, some just on the edges, and some completely.

Cheese Rolls

μπουρέκια με τυρί
MBOUREKIA ME TYRI

Kukla's soufflé-like filling inside these phyllo rolls is heavenly. Perfect to serve as a meze, for brunch, or as a side dish. Pair them with her Meat Rolls, as we did (pictured on opposite page), for a two-tone presentation. (For tips on how to work with phyllo, see Greek Cooking Techniques, page 43.)

FILLING
2 cups crumbled firm feta cheese
   (about 10 ounces)
½ cup warm Béchamel Sauce
   (recipe below)
2 extra-large egg yolks
½ teaspoon freshly grated nutmeg
¼ teaspoon white pepper

27 to 30 (14-by-18-inch) sheets
   #4 or #5 phyllo dough, at room
   temperature
½ cup butter, melted

BÉCHAMEL SAUCE
1 cup whole milk, divided
3 tablespoons cornstarch
½ tablespoon butter
Pinch fine sea salt
Pinch freshly ground pepper
⅓ cup grated *kefalotyri* cheese (or
   Parmigiano-Reggiano)
1 large egg, lightly beaten

KOUZINA TIP

EGGS KUKLA This is an elegant way to serve breakfast and use leftover Béchamel Sauce (there should be enough sauce for 4 to 6 eggs). Assemble on serving plates as follows: *Lightly toasted mini-pita round or brioche half* topped with *sautéed spinach, a poached egg, about 2 tablespoons Béchamel Sauce,* and *a sprig of fresh dill.* For a heartier dish, add *zampon (ham), smoked salmon,* or *steamed shellfish (snow crab legs, lobster claws, or shrimp).*

PREP TIME 50 minutes (includes cooking Béchamel Sauce)
BAKING TIME 30 to 35 minutes
DIFFICULTY LEVEL moderate
MAKES 18 to 20 rolls

1. *Make filling:* In a large bowl, stir together all of the filling ingredients until combined well. Makes about 2 cups of filling.

2. Arrange 2 racks in the center of the oven and heat to 350°F. Place the phyllo on your work surface with the wide end facing you. Vertically cut the phyllo stack in half, measuring 9-by-14 inches, and combine into 1 stack. Cover the phyllo with plastic wrap and a damp kitchen towel, keeping it covered while you work.

3. Working quickly, place 1 sheet of phyllo on your work surface with the narrow end facing you and lightly brush with butter. Repeat two more times for a total of 3 sheets, brushing each with butter. Place 1½ tablespoons of filling on the end closest to you and shape the filling into an oblong, leaving a 1-inch border on the end and on each side. Fold the end border over the filling, then fold in the sides and brush them with butter. Gently fold the filled section over and roll it to the end, taking care not to roll too tightly as this can cause the rolls to burst while baking. Lightly brush all of the sides with butter and place the roll, seam side down, on an ungreased large heavy-duty rimmed baking sheet. Repeat with the remaining phyllo, butter, and filling, placing the rolls 1 inch apart on the sheet. Bake until golden and puffed, 30 to 35 minutes. Serve hot.

BÉCHAMEL SAUCE
In a measuring cup, combine ½ cup milk and the cornstarch and stir until dissolved (the cornstarch will settle at the bottom, so stir again before using). In a heavy saucepan, bring the remaining ½ cup milk, the butter, salt, and pepper to a boil over medium-high heat. Remove from heat and, using a wooden spoon, stir in the dissolved cornstarch mixture until smooth. Cook over medium heat, stirring constantly, until the sauce thickens, about 5 minutes. Remove from heat and stir in the cheese until combined. Gradually stir in the egg, stirring rapidly while adding, until smooth. Set aside ½ cup of Béchamel Sauce for the Cheese Rolls recipe and reserve the remaining sauce for another use, like spooning over poached eggs (see KOUZINA TIP, left) or vegetables. *(This sauce can be refrigerated in an airtight container up to 2 days.)*

Meat Rolls

μπουρέκια με κιμά
MBOUREKIA ME KIMA

Kukla's favorite seasoning for meat, mbahari (allspice), lightly scents this filling, while onion, white wine, and tomatoes lend it rich flavor. (For tips on how to work with phyllo, see Greek Cooking Techniques, page 43.)

FILLING
2 tablespoons butter
1 tablespoon extra-virgin olive oil
2 cups finely chopped onion (about 1 large onion, 1 pound)
1 teaspoon fine sea salt, divided
½ teaspoon freshly ground pepper
1 pound lean ground beef
½ cup canned crushed tomatoes in thick puree
¼ cup semi-dry white wine
¼ cup water
⅛ teaspoon allspice (*mbahari*)
1 large egg, lightly beaten
⅓ cup grated *kefalotyri* cheese (or Parmigiano-Reggiano)

38 (14-by-18-inch) sheets #4 phyllo dough, at room temperature
½ cup plus 2 tablespoons butter, melted

PREP TIME 40 minutes plus standing
COOKING TIME 45 minutes
BAKING TIME 30 to 35 minutes
DIFFICULTY LEVEL moderate
MAKES 25 rolls

1. *Make filling:* In a large saucepot, melt together the butter and oil over medium-high heat. Add the onion, reduce heat to medium, and sauté, stirring occasionally, until softened, 5 to 7 minutes. Season with ½ teaspoon salt and the pepper, and cook until just golden, about 10 minutes. Add the ground beef and the remaining ½ teaspoon salt. Increase the heat to medium-high and cook, breaking up well with the back of a wooden spoon, until the beef is completely browned and any liquid is absorbed, 8 to 10 minutes. Stir in the tomatoes, wine, water, and allspice. Cover and simmer over medium-low heat until the liquid is absorbed, about 15 minutes. Remove from heat and let stand until the mixture has cooled to warm. Stir in the egg until combined well, then stir in the cheese. Makes about 2⅓ cups of filling.

2. Arrange 2 racks in the center of the oven and heat to 350°F. Place the phyllo on your work surface with the wide end facing you. Vertically cut the phyllo stack in half, measuring 9-by-14 inches, and combine into 1 stack. Cover the phyllo with plastic wrap and a damp kitchen towel, keeping it covered while you work.

3. Working quickly, place 1 sheet of phyllo on your work surface with the narrow end facing you and lightly brush with butter. Repeat two more times for a total of 3 sheets, brushing each with butter. Place 1½ tablespoons of filling on the end closest to you and shape the filling into an oblong, leaving a 1-inch border on the end and on each side. Fold the end border over the filling, then fold in the sides and brush them with butter. Gently fold the filled section over and roll it to the end, taking care not to roll too tightly as this can cause the rolls to burst while baking. Lightly brush all of the sides with butter and place the roll, seam side down, on an ungreased large heavy-duty rimmed baking sheet. Repeat with the remaining phyllo, butter, and filling, placing the rolls 1 inch apart on the sheet. Bake until golden and puffed, 30 to 35 minutes. *(Can be made ahead. Cool completely, then transfer to an airtight container, each layer separated by waxed paper, seal, and refrigerate up to 24 hours. Reheat rolls on a baking sheet in a preheated 350°F oven until heated through, about 15 minutes.)* Serve hot.

Phyllo Cheese Triangles
τυροπιτάκια τρίγωνα με φύλλο
TYROPITAKIA TRIGONA ME FILLO

Our phyllo *tyropitakia* are crisp on the outside and sumptuously cheesy inside. This crowd-pleaser meze can be prepared ahead and frozen before baking, making it perfect for last-minute get-togethers. Kukla's guests always wondered when she had time to do it all–this was her best-kept secret, and now, it's yours! (For tips on how to work with phyllo, see *Greek Cooking Techniques*, page 43.)

FILLING
8 ounces feta cheese, crumbled
8 ounces creamy small-curd
 cottage cheese or ricotta
¼ cup *each* grated kasseri and
 kefalotyri cheeses (or
 Parmigiano-Reggiano)
¼ cup finely chopped scallion
 (about 2 scallions)
2 ½ tablespoons chopped fresh dill
 (about 5 sprigs)
¼ teaspoon freshly grated nutmeg
2 extra-large eggs, lightly beaten
¼ cup plain dry bread crumbs

42 to 45 (9-by-14-inch) sheets
 #4 phyllo dough, at room
 temperature
¼ cup butter, melted

PREP TIME 1 hour
BAKING TIME 30 to 35 minutes
DIFFICULTY LEVEL moderate
MAKES 42 to 45 triangles

1. *Make filling:* In a medium bowl, combine the cheeses, scallion, and dill. Stir in the nutmeg, then the eggs, until combined well. Add the bread crumbs and stir until combined (the mixture should be the consistency of thick oatmeal). Makes 2 ⅔ cups of filling.

2. Arrange 2 racks in the center of the oven and heat to 350°F. Place the phyllo on your work surface with the narrow end facing you. Vertically cut the phyllo stack in half, measuring 4 ½-by-14 inches, and combine into 1 stack. Cover the phyllo with plastic wrap and a damp kitchen towel, keeping it covered while you work.

3. Working quickly, place 1 sheet of phyllo on your work surface with the narrow end facing you and lightly brush with butter. Cover with 1 more sheet and lightly brush with butter. Place 1 tablespoon of filling on the end closest to you, leaving a 1-inch border on the end. Fold one corner of the phyllo up around the filling to cover, forming a triangle, and flatten slightly in the center. Continue folding, flag-style, to the end of the phyllo. Trim any phyllo overhang with a sharp knife and lightly brush all of the sides with butter. Place the triangle, seam side down, on an ungreased large heavy-duty rimmed baking sheet. Repeat with the remaining phyllo, butter, and filling, placing the triangles 1 inch apart on the sheet. *(Can be made ahead. Arrange the unbaked triangles in an airtight container, each layer separated by waxed paper, seal, pressing out air, and freeze up to 2 weeks. Do not thaw before baking. Continue with recipe when ready to bake.)* Bake until golden and puffed, 30 to 35 minutes. *(Can be made ahead. Cool completely, then transfer the baked triangles to an airtight container, each layer separated by waxed paper. Cover with a paper towel, seal, pressing out air, and refrigerate up to 24 hours. Reheat triangles on a baking sheet in a preheated 350°F oven until heated through, about 15 minutes.)* Serve hot.

Petite Plates

Fried Greek Cheese Flambé

σαγανάκι
SAGANAKI

A *saganaki* is a small frying pan—though sometimes a larger pan is used depending on the number of servings—and anything cooked in it is called *saganaki*. This cheese *saganaki* is fried until crisp on the outside and soft on the inside. Drizzling with aromatic liquor to create a light flame (non-flaming method yields similar results), and flavoring with lemon juice, makes our *saganaki* not only delicious but a truly Greek meze. We like using brandy with the *kefalograviera* cheese and ouzo with the *halloumi*—either combination works well, so go with what tastes best for you.

1 large egg
Flour, for dusting
8 ounces *kefalograviera* or *halloumi* cheese, cut lengthwise into 4 slices (about ½ inch thick)
2 tablespoons virgin or extra-virgin olive oil
1½ tablespoons Greek brandy (such as Metaxa) or ouzo
1½ tablespoons fresh lemon juice (from ½ lemon)
Baby spring lettuce leaves or fresh oregano sprigs and lemon slices, for garnish

PREP TIME 5 minutes
COOKING TIME 6 minutes
DIFFICULTY LEVEL easy (*non-flaming* method)
SERVES 4 to 6

1. In a shallow bowl, beat the egg. In another shallow bowl, place about 2 tablespoons of flour. Dip the cheese slices in egg, letting the excess drip back into the bowl, then coat on all sides with flour, shaking off the excess back into the bowl. Transfer the coated cheese to a cookie sheet lined with parchment or waxed paper.

2. In a large cast-iron skillet, heat the oil over medium heat. Fry the cheese slices 2 to 2 ½ minutes per side until the edges are just golden. Proceed with your choice of *non-flaming* or *flaming* method below, then immediately go to step 3 to serve (the juices in the hot skillet dry up quickly, so transferring to serving plates right away is important).

NON-FLAMING METHOD Remove the skillet from the heat and, standing back, carefully add the brandy or ouzo (the liquor will steam and sizzle) and let stand just until most of the liquor has evaporated, about 30 seconds.

FLAMING METHOD See *warning* (left). Remove the skillet from the heat and, standing back, carefully add the brandy or ouzo (the liquor will steam and sizzle). While standing back and being very careful, immediately return the skillet to medium-high heat, tipping the skillet slightly by lifting the handle end just a little, to flame (if you have an electric or induction stovetop, ignite off the heat with a long-reach match or long-reach click lighter and continue, placing the skillet over low heat). Reduce to low heat and slide the skillet back and forth just until most of the liquor has evaporated and the flame has gone out, about 10 seconds. Remove the skillet from the heat.

3. Immediately transfer the fried cheese with the pan juices to warmed serving plates and drizzle with the lemon juice. Garnish with lettuce leaves or oregano sprigs and lemon slices, if desired. Serve hot.

WARNING

Flaming foods with alcohol can be dangerous and requires using extreme caution. Don't ignite near anything flammable and always have a fire extinguisher in the kitchen by your work area. This recipe allows you to achieve the same results whether you flame or not, and we give directions for both. We don't recommend flaming if you have no experience in this area or if you are uncomfortable using this method. Proceed at your own risk.

Greek Shrimp Cocktail
γαρίδες με σάλτσα κοκτέιλ
GARIDES ME SALTSA KOKTEIL

Loving shrimp as much as she did, Kukla set out to develop the perfect cocktail sauce (with help from her brother Bill) and she succeeded far beyond her own expectations— so much so that our aunts and uncles were thrilled when she would serve her Greek-style shrimp in her grand presentations. The cocktail sauce also goes well with steamed crab claws and fried calamari. This recipe serves eight generously but will easily feed up to 10, especially when accompanied by other meze plates or preceding dinner.

1½ lemons, cut into thick slices
1½ tablespoons fine sea salt
5 whole peppercorns
3 bay leaves
3 pounds jumbo shrimp (16 to 20 count)

COCKTAIL SAUCE
1 bottle (12 ounces) good-quality chili sauce
1¼ cups (10 ounces) good-quality ketchup
1½ tablespoons fresh lemon juice (from ½ lemon)
1½ teaspoons prepared horseradish (adding more or less, to taste)
1 teaspoon extra-virgin olive oil
½ teaspoon fine sea salt
⅛ teaspoon freshly ground pepper
Pinch sugar

8 to 10 leaves Boston lettuce or kale
4 to 5 small whole pineapples, cut in half lengthwise and fruit scooped out (or 8 to 10 cocktail bowls)

PREP TIME 30 minutes (includes 20 minutes for peeling and deveining shrimp), plus standing and chilling
COOKING TIME about 25 minutes
DIFFICULTY LEVEL easy
SERVES 8 to 10 (makes about 3 cups sauce)

1. Bring a large pot of water to a boil (about 1½ gallons) over medium-high heat. Add the lemon slices, salt, peppercorns, and bay leaves. Reduce heat to medium-low and simmer for 10 minutes. Increase heat and return to a boil. Stir in the shrimp, return to a boil, and cook just until opaque and the shells are bright pink, 1½ to 2 minutes (do not overcook); drain (if desired, reserve the cooking liquid as noted in KOUZINA TIP below). Let stand until cool enough to handle, then remove the shells from the shrimp, leaving the tails on, and devein. Transfer the shrimp to an airtight container and refrigerate at least 1 hour or overnight.

2. *Meanwhile, make Cocktail Sauce:* In a medium bowl, stir together all of the sauce ingredients until combined well. Cover and chill at least 1 hour before serving. *(Can be made ahead. Cover and refrigerate up to 2 days.)*

3. *To serve:* For a decorative presentation, place a lettuce leaf in each pineapple half or bowl (if serving in pineapples, top each leaf with a custard cup, if desired), and fill the center of each with Cocktail Sauce. Arrange the shrimp around the edges with the tail on the outside.

KOUZINA TIP

To save time, purchase flash-frozen raw shrimp that have already been peeled (with the tails left on) and deveined. Thaw according to package directions before cooking. If desired, reserve the cooking liquid to make a shrimp-flavored pilaf.

Stuffed Mushrooms

γεμιστά μανιτάρια
GEMISTA MANITARIA

Kukla needed an extra meze for a special occasion but she wanted to make something different, so she combined some of her favorite ingredients to whip up a stuffing for mushrooms. With these scrumptious gems, it's hard to eat just one, or two, so in the end you might be the one that's stuffed!

24 large white mushrooms, cleaned, stems removed and reserved

FILLING
2 tablespoons butter
1 tablespoon minced onion
¾ cup plain dry bread crumbs
¼ cup freshly grated *kefalograviera* cheese (or Parmigiano-Reggiano)
3 tablespoons chopped walnuts
1 tablespoon good-quality steak sauce
¼ teaspoon fine sea salt

1½ tablespoons butter, cut into 24 pieces, for dotting mushrooms

PREP TIME 35 minutes
COOKING TIME 5 minutes
BAKING TIME 20 to 25 minutes
DIFFICULTY LEVEL easy
MAKES 24 stuffed mushrooms

1. *Make filling:* Chop the reserved mushroom stems. In a medium skillet, melt the 2 tablespoons of butter over medium heat. Add the chopped mushroom stems and the onion and sauté until the onion is golden, about 4 minutes. Remove from heat. In a large bowl, combine the bread crumbs, cheese, walnuts, steak sauce, and salt. Add the mushroom-onion mixture and stir until combined well. Makes 1½ cups.

2. Arrange a rack in the center of the oven and heat to 400°F. Stuff each mushroom cap with about 1 tablespoon of filling and place them in a large shallow nonstick or lightly oiled baking dish. Add 1 tablespoon of water to the dish and dot each mushroom with 1 piece of the cut-up butter. Bake the stuffed mushrooms until lightly golden around the edges, 20 to 25 minutes. *(Can be made ahead. Cool completely, then transfer to an airtight container, in a single layer, seal, pressing out air, and refrigerate up to 24 hours. Reheat stuffed mushrooms on a rimmed baking sheet in a preheated 350°F oven until heated through, about 10 minutes.)* Serve hot.

Ham Canapés

κανапέ με ζαμπόν

KANAPE ME ZAMPON

Kukla's response to deviled eggs, this festive meze is deceptively easy to make and can be prepared up to one day ahead. Versatile enough to go from brunch to dinner, this hearty appetizer will fill out your menu nicely.

FILLING

4 large eggs, hard-boiled, cooled, and peeled
2 tablespoons butter, softened
¾ teaspoon spicy brown mustard
2 teaspoons finely chopped dill pickle, patted dry with paper towels
⅛ teaspoon fine sea salt
Pinch freshly ground pepper

6 slices (⅛ inch thick) Black Forest deli ham

Chopped pimento, dill pickle (patted dry), and/or roasted orange bell pepper, for garnish

TOTAL PREP TIME 15 minutes plus chilling
DIFFICULTY LEVEL easy
SERVES 6

1. *Make filling:* Cut the eggs in half and separate the yolks from the whites. Finely chop the whites and set aside. In a food processor, pulse together the yolks, butter, and mustard until smooth. Transfer the yolk mixture to a medium bowl and stir in the chopped egg whites, the 2 teaspoons pickle, the salt, and pepper until combined. Transfer the filling to a pastry bag with a 1-inch opening (or to a heavy-duty plastic storage bag with one corner snipped to 1-inch diameter).

2. Roll the ham slices into the shape of cones and secure the seams with toothpicks (or tie a thin carrot ribbon or the green leaf of a scallion around the outside center of each). Pipe the filling into the center of each cone, filling them completely. Refrigerate the canapés at least 1 hour to set and chill before serving. *(Can be made ahead. Transfer to an airtight container and refrigerate up to 24 hours.)*

3. *To serve:* Carefully remove the toothpicks from the cones and arrange the canapés on a serving platter. Garnish with chopped pimento, pickle, and/or bell pepper, if desired. Serve chilled.

KOUZINA TIP

Choose the garnish color that best suits your occasion. Red pimento and green pickle are perfect for the holidays, while chopped roasted orange bell pepper is ideal for fall.

Cocktail Meatballs

κεφτεδάκια
KEFTEDAKIA

A delicious meze, our herbed mini meatballs are light and moist, and can be served alone, with lemon wedges, or with the perfect accompaniment, Yogurt-Cucumber Sauce/Dip (Tzatziki, page 17). These meatballs can also be made with ground lamb or a combination of beef and lamb. Pictured on opposite page with Tzatziki.

½ cup all-purpose flour, for rolling

MEATBALLS
2 pounds lean ground beef (such as sirloin)
1½ cups finely chopped onion (about 2 medium onions, ¾ pound)
¾ cup plain dry bread crumbs
½ cup water
¼ cup chopped fresh flat-leaf parsley (4 to 5 sprigs)
1 extra-large egg
1 tablespoon minced garlic (about 6 cloves)
1 tablespoon extra-virgin olive oil
2 teaspoons dried mint or 3 tablespoons finely chopped fresh mint
1½ teaspoons fine sea salt
1 teaspoon dried oregano
1 teaspoon baking powder
¼ teaspoon freshly ground pepper

Vegetable oil, for frying

Lemon wedges, optional
Yogurt-Cucumber Sauce/Dip (Tzatziki, page 17), optional

PREP TIME 20 minutes
COOKING TIME about 30 minutes
DIFFICULTY LEVEL easy
MAKES about 80 meatballs

1. Place the flour in a shallow bowl or pie plate. Set aside.

2. In a large bowl, using your hands, mix together all of the meatball ingredients just until combined. Do not over-handle as this can make the meatballs tough. Using 1 tablespoon of meatball mixture for each, shape into 1-inch balls, roll them in the flour, shaking off the excess back into the bowl. Transfer the floured meatballs to a large cookie sheet lined with parchment or waxed paper.

3. In a small deep saucepot, heat 1½ inches of vegetable oil over medium heat to 375°F on a deep-fry thermometer. Add 5 or 6 meatballs at a time to the hot oil and cook until browned, 1 to 2 minutes, adjusting the heat, if necessary, to maintain a temperature of 375°F. Using a slotted spoon, transfer the meatballs to a plate lined with paper towels to drain. Repeat the process with the remaining meatballs. *(Can be made ahead. Cool completely, then transfer to an airtight container and refrigerate up to 2 days. Reheat meatballs on a rimmed baking sheet, in a single layer, in a preheated 350°F oven until heated through, about 15 minutes.)* Transfer the meatballs to a serving platter and serve immediately with lemon wedges or Yogurt-Cucumber Sauce/Dip (*Tzatziki*), if desired.

Stuffed Grape Leaves

ντολμαδάκια με κληματόφυλλα
DOLMADAKIA ME KLIMATOFILLA

Traditionally these appetizers are made two ways, with meat and without (Gialantzi, recipe follows). Kukla developed perfect variations for both, this one featuring the addition of ground beef (ground lamb also works well) and an optional recipe for a special Avgolemono sauce made with broth from the cooked dolmadakia. (For tips on how to prepare and roll dolmadakia, see Greek Cooking Techniques, page 45.)

About 55 grape leaves (from a
   1-pound jar), drained

FILLING
⅓ cup extra-virgin olive oil
1 ¾ cups chopped onion (about
   1 large onion, ¾ pound)
½ cup thinly sliced scallion (about
   4 scallions)
Fine sea salt
1 pound lean ground beef (such
   as sirloin)
1 cup finely chopped fresh dill
   (about 1 small bunch)
½ cup canned whole plum
   tomatoes in thick puree, seeds
   removed and tomatoes chopped
½ cup long-grain converted rice,
   rinsed and drained
¼ cup chopped fresh flat-leaf
   parsley (4 to 5 sprigs)
1 extra-large egg, lightly beaten
⅛ teaspoon freshly ground pepper

Extra-virgin olive oil, for coating the
   pot
½ cup butter, cut up
1 lemon, one half cut into ¼-inch-
   thick slices
2 cups boiling water

AVGOLEMONO
(Egg-Lemon Sauce), optional
Broth from cooked *dolmadakia*
2 ½ tablespoons cornstarch
2 extra-large egg yolks
2 tablespoons fresh lemon juice
   (from 1 lemon)

Lemon slices or wedges, for serving

PREP TIME 1 hour 15 minutes, plus standing
COOKING TIME 1 hour
DIFFICULTY LEVEL easy to moderate
MAKES about 55 *dolmadakia*, serving 8 to 10

1. Fill a large pot halfway up the sides with water and bring it to a boil over medium-high heat. Remove the grape leaves from the jar, carefully unroll them, and rinse well under cool water. Gently separate the leaves into 3 batches. Carefully add the leaves, 1 batch at a time, to the boiling water, return to a boil, and blanch until the leaves turn bright green, 1 to 2 minutes. Using tongs, immediately transfer the leaves to a colander and rinse under cool water. Drain well, gently separate the leaves, and spread them out on a large plate, snipping off the tough stem extending from each leaf. (Set aside any torn or damaged leaves to line the bottom and top of the pot. When stuffing, small leaves can be used to patch torn ones by overlapping to cover the tear.) Set aside to cool.

2. *Meanwhile, make filling:* In a large skillet, heat the oil over medium heat. Add the onion and scallion, season with ⅛ teaspoon salt, and sauté, stirring occasionally, until lightly golden, about 20 minutes; cool slightly. In a large bowl, stir the onion mixture into the ground beef until combined. Add the dill, tomatoes, rice, parsley, egg, ¼ teaspoon salt, and the pepper. Stir until combined well. Set aside. Makes about 3 ⅓ cups.

3. Line the bottom of a heavy stockpot with some of the reserved damaged leaves (this will keep the stuffed leaves from sticking to the bottom and burning). Coat the sides of the pot with oil. Place 1 leaf on your work surface with the shiny side down and the stem-end closest to you. Place about 1 tablespoon of filling shaped in an oval on the stem end. Fold the leaf ends closest to you over the filling, covering it completely, then fold in the sides and roll to the end of the leaf. Place the stuffed leaf, seam side down, in the prepared pot. Repeat with the remaining leaves and filling, neatly and snugly arranging them around the pot in a circular pattern and stacking them in layers.

4. Evenly arrange the butter and lemon slices over the *dolmadakia*. Squeeze the remaining lemon half over the *dolmadakia* and arrange the reserved leaves on top, covering them completely. Cover with an inverted shallow heatproof bowl or pie plate. The bowl should be small enough so as not to touch the sides of the pot but large enough that it covers the *dolmadakia*. This will weigh them down and keep them

in place while cooking. Carefully pour the 2 cups of boiling water over the bowl. Cover the pot and simmer over low heat until the *dolmadakia* are cooked through and the leaves are tender, 15 to 20 minutes. If making *Avgolemono*, immediately follow the instruction in step 5 to strain the broth from the cooked *dolmadakia*. Serve warm or at room temperature with lemon slices and *Avgolemono*, if desired.

5. *Avgolemono:* Using potholders, hold the lid slightly askew over the pot with the *dolmadakia* (leaving the bowl in the pot). Carefully tilt the pot to pour the warm broth into a medium saucepan (you should have about 2 ⅓ cups broth). Set the broth aside to cool to lukewarm. Place the cornstarch on one side of a shallow bowl. Add the egg yolks to the other side of the bowl and stir just the yolks until combined. Gradually stir the cornstarch into the yolks, stirring in the lemon juice a little at a time to smooth the mixture. When completely combined and smooth, slowly stir in ½ cup lukewarm broth from the *dolmadakia* to temper the eggs. Slowly stir the egg-lemon mixture into the remaining broth in the saucepan. Cook over low heat, stirring constantly, until the sauce is thickened and smooth (it should be the consistency of hollandaise sauce), about 5 minutes. Makes 2 ½ cups.

KOUZINA TIP

When purchasing jarred grape leaves, look for those that are the lightest green—they're younger, making them more tender than the dark leaves. You can also use fresh grape leaves, again choosing the smaller, lighter, young leaves, available in May and June.

See *Greek Cooking Techniques:* Dolmadakia: How to Prepare and Roll, page 45, for how-to tips.

Meatless-Lenten Stuffed Grape Leaves

ντολμαδάκια γιαλαντζί-νηστίσιμα
DOLMADAKIA GIALANTZI-NISTISIMA

Kukla's meatless dolmadakia variation is usually eaten during Lent or other fasting periods, but they're so good it would be a shame to wait until then to serve them. (For tips on how to prepare and roll dolmadakia, see Greek Cooking Techniques, page 45.)

About 65 grape leaves (1-pound jar), drained

FILLING
½ cup extra-virgin olive oil
3 ½ cups coarsely grated onion (about 1 ½ pounds)
¼ cup thinly sliced scallion (about 2 scallions)
½ teaspoon fine sea salt, divided
2 ⅓ cups long-grain converted rice (from a 1-pound box)
½ cup chopped fresh flat-leaf parsley (about 10 sprigs)
3 tablespoons fresh lemon juice (from 1 lemon)
½ teaspoon dried mint leaves, crushed
⅛ teaspoon freshly ground pepper

½ cup extra-virgin olive oil, plus more for coating the pot
6 cups vegetable broth, divided
⅓ cup fresh lemon juice (from 2 lemons)

Lemon slices or wedges, for serving

PREP TIME 1 hour 20 minutes, plus standing
COOKING TIME 1 hour
DIFFICULTY LEVEL easy
MAKES about 65 *dolmadakia*, serving 12 to 15

1. Prepare the grape leaves as in step 1 of Stuffed Grape Leaves, page 40. Set aside.

2. *Meanwhile, make filling:* In a large skillet, heat the oil over medium heat. Add the onion and scallion, season with ¼ teaspoon salt, and sauté, stirring occasionally, until lightly golden, about 20 minutes. Remove from heat. Add the rice, parsley, 3 tablespoons lemon juice, the mint, remaining ¼ teaspoon salt, and the pepper, stirring after each ingredient is added to combine well. Set aside. Makes 4 ½ cups.

3. Line the bottom of a heavy stockpot with some of the reserved damaged leaves (this will keep the stuffed leaves from sticking to the bottom and burning). Coat the sides of the pot with oil. Place 1 leaf on your work surface with the shiny side down and the stem-end closest to you. Place about 1 tablespoon of filling shaped in an oval on the stem end. Fold the leaf ends closest to you over the filling, covering it completely, then fold in the sides and roll to the end of the leaf. Place the stuffed leaf, seam side down, in the prepared pot. Repeat with the remaining leaves and filling, neatly and snugly arranging them around the pot in a circular pattern and stacking them in layers.

4. In a large pot, bring the vegetable broth to a boil. Evenly pour 1 cup of hot broth and the ½ cup oil over the *dolmadakia*. Cover with an inverted shallow heatproof bowl or pie plate. The bowl should be small enough so as not to touch the sides of the pot but large enough that it covers the *dolmadakia*. This will weigh them down and keep them in place while cooking. Carefully pour the remaining 5 cups of hot broth over the bowl. Cover the pot and simmer over low heat until the rice is cooked and the leaves are tender, 25 minutes. Carefully remove the bowl and the leaves on top, evenly pour the ⅓ cup lemon juice over the *dolmadakia*, tightly cover the pot, and let cool completely. *(Can be made ahead. Transfer to an airtight container and refrigerate up to 3 days.)* Serve at room temperature, slightly chilled (refrigerate 3 hours), or cold (refrigerate overnight), with lemon slices or wedges.

GREEK COOKING TECHNIQUES

Specific techniques used throughout this cookbook, such as *Phyllo: How to Work with It*, *Dolmadakia: How to Prepare and Roll*, and *Using a Goudi and Goudoheri*, are just some of the topics discussed in detail in this chapter and on our website's blog at *kuklaskouzina.com* (blog titles are included in each section). Our discussions include step-by-step instructions and images (on our blog) that demonstrate Kukla's shortcut tips and tricks, making it easy for the at-home cook to follow. Detailed information about food items discussed here can be found in the chapter *Kouzina A to Ω: Equipment, Ingredients, Common Cooking Methods & Food Terms of Greek Island Cuisine*.

PHYLLO (FILLO / FILO): HOW TO WORK WITH IT

Phyllo comes in a variety of sheet thicknesses, and as the phyllo number listed on the box goes up, so does the thickness, making #4 the thinnest and #10 the thickest. It's a mystery as to what happened to #1, #2, and #3, but we think that when phyllo makers originally assigned numbers, they wanted to leave room for thinner versions—if that's even possible. Read more about *phyllo* in *Kouzina A to Ω:* Ingredients, page 54, to decide which thickness fits your needs. Phyllo is also available in shredded (*kataifi*) and in prebaked shell forms.

Number 4 thin phyllo dough is the phyllo-sheet thickness we most use because it's perfect for everything from meze pastries to entrée pitas to syrup desserts, and the result is always flaky, lightly crisp, and flawless. It's been said that #4 is for intermediate to experienced bakers, but even a beginner can have success with a few simple (and doable) tips. If you're a little nervous about working with phyllo, you can start with #7 thick phyllo dough—you'll use fewer sheets than #4 but will need to apply a more liberal coating of butter or olive oil on each sheet to keep it from overdrying.

Phyllo also comes in a number of sheet sizes, so if you're making meze *Tyropitakia* you can use the smaller 9-by-14-inch sheets. For a tray pita the 12-by-17-inch and 14-by-18-inch sheets will give you greater coverage while allowing you to use fewer sheets.

10 STEPS AND TIPS TO FLAWLESS PHYLLO

Unlock the secrets of working with phyllo and make it work perfectly for you by following the 10 key steps and tips below, then do a test run before your big day of baking. This will help you to figure out in advance which market is reliable for buying the freshest phyllo. You'll also gain confidence as you become more familiar with the dough sheets.

1. *Buy it refrigerated or frozen?:* Phyllo leaves most factories frozen and should stay frozen until you purchase it. Phyllo doesn't respond well to being exposed to multiple temperature changes. Remember that phyllo is dough that has been rolled out to a super-thin thickness, making it extremely delicate. The freezer dries out dough, especially phyllo dough, if thawed and then re-frozen. Some markets sell phyllo in the refrigerator section—meaning they thawed it from a frozen state—in which case, keep it refrigerated and use it within a couple of days. We know the package instructions say to keep it frozen—but if you purchased it refrigerated and re-freeze it, it will most likely crack and fall apart as soon as you unwrap it. It's important to note that when phyllo sits in the refrigerator for more than a couple of days it will start to dry out around the edges and develop mold in the center. For this reason, some markets keep the phyllo frozen, then transfer it into the refrigerator section a little at a time so it won't go bad. Adding insult to injury, on their journey to your counter, some phyllo products start out frozen, are thawed in the refrigerator, and are then *re*-frozen before you purchase them—a nightmare even for an experienced baker. Can you tell we've been there, done that?

2. *Buy it fresh:* Get your phyllo a day or two before you're going to use it so it's at its freshest and most pliable. Shop at a market that has quick turnover when it comes to phyllo—if it does, you'll be able to avoid the freezer issue in step 1. How can you avoid being on the buying end of *re*-frozen phyllo? Unless someone tips you off about the market's practices, you can't. You'll buy it, figure out what happened, and then never buy phyllo at that market again. Plus, you'll be running out at the eleventh hour to get phyllo somewhere else. We've gone down that road and learned by trial and error where the good stuff is sold—you will too!

Ask the store manager if their frozen phyllo has been refrigerated and re-frozen. If it's a good store, they'll be honest with you, though they can't really vouch for how the phyllo was stored before they received it. Greek/Mediterranean shops sell items like phyllo quickly, so you can rely on the freshness of the product, especially if they always have a good flow of people shopping there. Some supermarkets carry a fresh supply, so you might have luck there as well.

3. *Thaw properly:* Bring the unopened package of phyllo to room temperature before using. If purchased refrigerated, thaw for ½ hour for sheets and 2 hours for *kataifi*; if frozen, thaw about 5 hours (or follow package directions). Cold phyllo will not be flexible and will crack, so this is really important. Prebaked shells can be used right from the freezer.

4. *Organize:* Prepare your filling while you're waiting for the phyllo to come to room temperature (a major time-saver). Melt your butter or heat your olive oil, and have your utensils ready: baking pan/tray, sharp-tipped knife, and a natural-bristle pastry brush (don't use silicone—it will stick to and tear the phyllo)—a large brush for pan-sized pies or a small one for individual items. Clean and thoroughly dry your work surface. Have a kitchen towel and plastic wrap ready to use (see step 6).

5. *Work quickly:* Phyllo dries out in seconds. *Seriously,* seconds! So it's important to have everything you need lined up and ready to go. If you're prepared, you're halfway there. Once you start working with the phyllo, work fast!

6. *Keep it covered:* This is especially important. After it comes to room temperature, take the phyllo out of the package and unroll it on a clean, DRY work surface (make sure it's completely dry or the phyllo will stick to it). Immediately place a sheet of plastic wrap and a damp kitchen towel (to weigh down the plastic wrap) over the phyllo, covering it completely. This will keep most of the air out and will prevent the phyllo from drying/cracking so it will remain pliable. When working with *kataifi*, remove it from the package, unroll it, and work with small quantities, leaving the remaining *kataifi* covered as you would phyllo sheets. Follow your recipe directions for brushing, rolling, layering, etc.

7. *Brushing and handling:* Though the basic method for working with phyllo is standard for most recipes, we also include some additional tips when it comes to making individual pieces as opposed to tray pitas.

> There are two basic rules when it comes to phyllo and brushing with butter or olive oil:
> 1. Sheets of phyllo should not be touching unless they have butter or oil between them (this is the glue).
> 2. The outer layer must be brushed completely with butter or olive oil.

Individual pieces: If you're making items like *Mbourekia* or *Tyropitakia*, using a sharp knife, cut the phyllo sheets in half or into thirds, as directed in the recipe, then assemble into one stack.

Place one sheet on your work surface and cover the remaining sheets. Using a small pastry brush, gently and lightly brush the sheet with melted butter or oil all the way to the edges. Cover with another sheet, brush again, and, if directed, repeat with one more sheet (2 to 3 sheets total, each brushed).

> NOTE: The above is if you're using #4 phyllo. Keep in mind that #4 phyllo requires a light touch with a pastry brush to avoid tearing. If you're using #7, you can do this with 2 sheets (instead of 3), brushing each layer and the outside with more butter or oil than you would with #4. We don't recommend using #10 sheets for *mezedes*, as their thickness would result in a hard crust. If the recipe calls for a specific phyllo thickness, then use the number of sheets it recommends. If a thickness is not given, #4 is the standard.

> *To make a triangle:* Place the filling on one end of the prepared phyllo and fold one corner over to cover the filling, flatten slightly in the center, then continue to fold, flag-style, to the end of the phyllo. Trim off any overhang.

> *To make a roll:* Place the filling centered on one end of the prepared phyllo and fold over enough phyllo on the end to cover the filling. Fold in the sides, brush them with butter or oil, and roll to the end of the phyllo.

> Do not fold or roll the pieces tightly, or the filling will burst out while baking. Leave just a little wiggle room.

> Brush the pieces all over with butter or oil, then place, seam side down, on an ungreased baking sheet.

8. *Patching:* Be careful not to tear the sheets when you're working. But if you do, and the tear is obvious, overlap the torn phyllo edges if you can, or cover the tear with a strip of phyllo, always brushing butter or oil between each sheet. Keep in mind that once phyllo sheets are joined with butter or oil they're pretty much glued, so if you need to separate them to repair a tear and they won't budge, leave them alone before it becomes a bigger mess. The best thing to do is to brush the torn sheet with butter or oil and cover it with another sheet. No one will notice the tear if the top sheet looks good.

9. *Shells (do-ahead tips):* Mini and large prebaked frozen phyllo shells can be used right from the freezer—no thawing required. Prepare your filling ahead and assemble and/or bake as follows:

For no-bake recipes: Fill the shells up to 3 hours ahead (any longer could make the shells soggy) and keep them refrigerated until you're ready to serve.

For bake recipes: First lightly brush the inside of the shells with olive oil (they tend to be dry if you don't), then spoon in your favorite savory or sweet filling. The shells can be filled up to 3 hours ahead and kept refrigerated. Bake them in a preheated oven according to recipe directions just before serving.

10. *Spray option:* This is the ultimate tip for phyllo-phobes. If you're not fast with a brush, or have always had a problem with phyllo tearing on you, this tip is custom-made for you. Use olive oil in a spray can. You can find it at most markets or you can buy a refillable spray bottle and fill it with your favorite olive oil. Lightly spray the oil directly on the phyllo wherever the instructions call for brushing. It's quick so the phyllo doesn't have time to dry out. Brushing is best since you have more control over how much butter or oil is applied, but, if you need an easier option, this is the next best thing.

(To learn more about *phyllo*, see *Kouzina A to Ω: Ingredients*, page 54.)

For more on phyllo and images for the above, visit our website:
Fillo (Phyllo): Learn How to Work with It and Bake Beautifully

DOLMADAKIA: HOW TO PREPARE AND ROLL

Dolmadakia and *Dolmadakia Gialantzi* are small dolma made with grape leaves and are served as a meze. Following are our detailed directions and insider tips on how to approach *dolmadakia* that will help you make your meze authentic every time.

Grape leaves (known as *klimatofilla* or *ambelofilla*) for *dolmadakia* can either be picked fresh or purchased brined in a jar, the latter being the most common (see *Kouzina A to Ω: Ingredients: Grape Leaves*, page 51). The following preparation works for both jarred and fresh leaves.

PREPARATION FOR LEAVES

1. Fill a large pot halfway up the sides with water and bring it to a boil over medium-high heat. Meanwhile, remove the leaves from the jar and carefully unroll them but do not separate the leaves. Rinse the leaves well under cool water (to remove the brine). Gently separate the leaves into 3 batches. Carefully add the leaves, 1 batch at a time, to the boiling water, return it to a boil, and blanch the leaves until they turn bright green, 1 to 2 minutes. Using tongs, immediately transfer the leaves to a colander and rinse under cool water. Drain well. Gently separate and transfer the leaves to a large plate, snipping off the tough stem extending from each leaf. Handle the leaves gently to avoid tearing. Set aside and reserve any torn or damaged leaves to line the bottom and top of your pot. When stuffing, small leaves can be used to patch torn ones by simply overlapping to cover the tear.

2. When the leaves are cool enough to handle, line the bottom of a large heavy stockpot with a layer of the reserved damaged leaves. This will keep the *dolmadakia* from touching the bottom of the pot and burning.

FILL AND ROLL

1. Working with one leaf at a time, arrange the leaf, shiny side down, on your work surface and place the filling, as directed in the recipe, on the stem end of the leaf. Fold the leaf ends closest to you over the filling, covering the filling completely. Fold in the sides, then roll to the end of the leaf. Place the stuffed leaf, seam side down, in your prepared pot.

2. As you fill the pot with the *dolmadakia*, make sure they are placed neatly and snugly against each other in each layer so they don't move while cooking. When the pot is full, follow the recipe for the amount of broth and any flavorings to add. Arrange the reserved damaged leaves on top, covering the *dolmadakia* completely.

COOK
Cover the top of the *dolmadakia* in the pot with an inverted shallow heatproof bowl or pie plate. The bowl should be small enough so as not to touch the sides of the pot but large enough that it covers the *dolmadakia*. The bowl will keep the *dolmadakia* from rising to the top of the pot and unraveling while cooking, and will ensure that they cook properly. Follow the recipe for the remaining cooking directions.

SERVE
Once cooked, *dolmadakia* can be served warm or at room temperature with lemon slices and/or *Avgolemono* (Egg-Lemon Sauce), page 40, though some people enjoy them cold.

Dolmadakia are typically served with feta, kalamata olives, and assorted dips. For a meze party, pair *dolmadakia* with ouzo, or a semi-dry white or rosé wine.

(To learn more about *dolmadakia*, see *Kouzina A to Ω: Food Terms*, page 59.)

For more on *dolmadakia* and images for the above, visit our website:
Greek Dolmades: Stuff, Wrap & Roll

HOW TO MAKE GREEK YOGURT
When yogurt is called for in Greek cooking, it is drained (strained) Greek sheep's-milk yogurt, which is the consistency of cream cheese. Sheep's-milk yogurt is sweeter and creamier than cow's-milk and is available in Greek markets and gourmet shops. You can also use thick Mediterranean-style sheep's-milk or cow's-milk yogurt (like Fage) available in supermarkets and specialty food stores throughout the United States. Homemade drained yogurt is a good substitute and simple to make. The following recipe will produce a thick yogurt that you can eat plain, topped with fruit and honey, or use in recipes calling for Greek yogurt.

To make 1 cup of drained yogurt:
16 ounces (2 cups) plain (unflavored) whole-milk yogurt

Line a fine mesh sieve with a double thickness of cheesecloth and place it over a large bowl. Place the yogurt in the cheesecloth, gather up the sides, and tie them together with kitchen twine. Cover the bowl with plastic wrap and let the yogurt drain in the refrigerator 2 to 4 hours or overnight (discard the water collected in the bowl).

(To learn more about Greek *yogurt*, see *Kouzina A to Ω: Ingredients*, page 58.)

USING A GOUDI AND GOUDOHERI (MORTAR AND PESTLE)
We use a solid brass *goudi* and *goudoheri* to chop foods that need a heavier hand like nuts, seeds, and mastic. The weighty *goudoheri* helps you in your task, and you don't have to pound as hard. Working in batches, place about ¼ cup or less of the food in the *goudi*, cover the opening with one hand or a towel, and pound up and down with the *goudoheri* until you reach the desired result.

The wooden *goudi* and *goudoheri*, with its wider *goudoheri* end and larger *goudi* bowl surface, is great for mashing softer foods like garlic and for grinding herbs. Instead of pounding, firmly press down on the food with the *goudoheri* and twist. Repeat pressing and twisting until you reach the desired result.

(To learn more about the *goudi* and *goudoheri*, see *Kouzina A to Ω: Equipment*, page 47.)

KOUZINA A TO Ω

EQUIPMENT, INGREDIENTS, COMMON COOKING METHODS & FOOD TERMS OF GREEK ISLAND CUISINE

The *goudi*, *briki*, and *tapsi* are just a few of the items that are unique to the **equipment** used in the Greek *kouzina*. In this section we'll discuss these and many more, including their uses, so you can familiarize yourself with the utensils and cooking/baking vessels that you should have on hand for your *Meze* journey with us.

Ingredients, such as *kefalograviera* and *tarama*, are not only defined in depth, from their origins to their flavors and textures to the various ways they're used in Greek cooking, but also provided are comparable substitutions where applicable.

Common cooking methods, like *avgolemono* and *gemista*, will help you recognize the style of a dish from its title and will demonstrate how the standard ingredients in Greek island cooking are combined and adapted to create added dimensions to this beloved cuisine.

Greek **food terms** like *houfta* and *preza* are listed and described in this section, taking some of the guesswork out of Yiayia's handwritten recipes, while other terms like *kaimaki* and *ladera* tell you about the food elements. This is where you'll also learn about the difference between a *taverna* and an *ouzeri*.

In the following chapter, *Greek Food & Product Sources*, page 62, you'll find a list of markets and online sources where you can purchase Greek kitchen equipment and ingredients.

EQUIPMENT

The must-have tools of the Greek kouzina are sometimes universal and at other times unique to this cuisine. We've broken down the most-used equipment and utensils that you should have available to re-create our recipes.

BRIKI (μπρίκι, BREE-kee): DEMITASSE COFFEEPOT
Traditionally made of brass or copper and lined with tin, the briki (or *ibrik* in Turkish) has a long handle that is usually angled upward and is used to make Greek coffee (see *Food Terms:* Ellinikos kafes). Modern versions for everyday use come in stainless steel. Sizes typically range from the small 2-serving briki to a large 4-serving briki. This pot's deep, wider base and narrowing shape allows the coffee to form more of a *kaimaki* (see *Food Terms*), or foam, at the top.

ELEODOHEO / ELEODOXEO (ελαιοδοχείο, eh-leh-oh-thoh-HEE-oh): OLIVE OIL CAN / DECANTER
Perfect for keeping a small amount of oil (about 2 cups) handy for drizzling on salads or measuring by the spoonful. The spout dispenses the oil slowly so you have more control when pouring.

GOUDI AND GOUDOHERI (γουδί και γουδοχέρι, yoo-THEE keh yoo-thoh-HEH-ree): MORTAR AND PESTLE
Goudi is the term commonly used to refer to both the mortar and pestle. The goudi, a staple in the Greek kouzina, is the original Greek food processor. It is most commonly found in brass, marble, and wood forms. For centuries it has been used to mash garlic into a paste for Skordalia, pound mahlepi (mahleb/mahlab/mahaleb) into a powder for tsoureki (Greek Pascha/Easter bread), and evenly chop nuts for pastries. This method may sound outdated compared to today's electric appliances but the goudi is irreplaceable when it comes to precise processing because you can control the pressure applied, as well as where to apply it. If you ever used an electric food processor to chop nuts, you probably ended up with some chopped, some barely chopped, and some ground. In the time it takes to remove this mix of textures from the processor, then return the large nut pieces to re-chop, you could have uniformly chopped all of the nuts using a goudi. We use a wooden goudi and goudoheri for garlic and a brass one for everything else to avoid having the pungent garlic smell and taste transfer to other foods. (See *Greek Cooking Techniques:* Using a Goudi and Goudoheri, page 46.)

PINELO (πινέλο, pee-NEH-loh): NATURAL-BRISTLE PASTRY BRUSH
When working with *phyllo* (see *Ingredients*), this pastry brush is a must-have. We recommend two sizes, a 1-inch for mini pitas and a 2-inch for large ones and for greasing pans. Make sure you use a natural-bristle brush, not silicone, as silicone will stick to and tear delicate phyllo.

PLASTIS (πλάστης, PLAH-stees): LONG, THIN, STRAIGHT ROLLING PIN
For rolling out pastry dough like a homemade phyllo or multilayered Karpathian baklava, this 20- to 40-inch rolling pin is indispensable. Kukla (Mom) used an old broomstick (minus the broom) that our yiayia had sanded and cleaned (in Karpathos this rolling pin is called a xyliki, ξυλίκι, ksee-LEE-kee). It was the perfect size for the large-scale baking they did.

SOUROTIRI (σουρωτήρι, soo-roh-TEE-ree): MESH STRAINER FOR FRYING AND DRAINING
When making fried pastries, a small sourotiri with a long handle is needed to quickly remove them from the oil while draining them in the process. A large sourotiri is similar to a fine-mesh sieve and is used to strain and remove lumps from sauces and custards. A colander is also referred to as a sourotiri.

TAPSI (ταψί, tah-PSEE): PAN / BAKING SHEET
The essential round heavy-duty, stainless-steel baking pan (never nonstick) that comes in various sizes is the tapsi, which is used for making spanakopita, moussaka, roasted lamb and potatoes, galaktomboureko, and numerous other dishes.

Tapsi also refers to a heavy-duty, stainless-steel rimmed baking sheet (also never nonstick). Rimless cookie sheets are not good for Greek baking because the ingredients in pastries and cookies include a lot of butter and/or oil that can drip off the sheet while baking if there's no rim.

Heavy-duty is key to keep food from burning on the bottom before the center and top have cooked through, and to prevent delicate pastries from over-browning.

ZYGARIA (ζυγαριά, zee-yahr-YAH): FOOD SCALE
Much of Greek cooking includes ingredients that are measured in kilos or pounds (like flour), making a food scale a must. We have two: our mom's from the 1950s and our yiayia's brass balancing scale from the 1920s. Both still work perfectly and are really cool antique conversation pieces—practical as well as decorative!

INGREDIENTS

The ingredients listed here may not all be unique to Greece but each is considered a staple in the Greek kouzina, and their various pairings (see *Common Cooking Methods*) are indigenous to the country's cuisine. When roasting meat with an olive oil, lemon, oregano, and garlic marinade, the aroma scenting the air in your kouzina and throughout your home will instantly make you think Greek. This is what defines our cooking style. Greeks know how to do food that everyone will recognize and can enjoy!

Greek cooking is simple when it comes to the elements of everyday foods. Always look for fresh, high-quality ingredients. There should be a balance in your meal, with spices and herbs adding flavor but never overpowering the main ingredient.

BOUILLON: ZOMOS (ζωμός, zoh-MOHS)
Bouillon is used throughout Greek cooking and gives a flavorful boost to a number of different meals. Bouillon cubes and powdered bouillon are a convenient way of adding savor to dishes without having to worry about a brief shelf life, as with broth and stock, plus they don't take up a lot of space in your pantry. Kukla incorporated bouillon cubes in a number of her dishes and stored the cubes in the refrigerator to keep them extra fresh. Wherever possible in our recipes, we offer a broth substitute as an option.

CHEESE: TYRI (τυρί, tee-REE)
Aside from the renowned feta, there's a wealth of Greek cheeses that are not well known in the non-Greek community. Most of these cheeses are widely used in our recipes, as well as served on a *meze* platter (see *Food Terms*). Though

they might seem unfamiliar, many of these cheeses are available in specialty markets, gourmet shops, Greek/Mediterranean stores, and supermarkets throughout the United States.

The Greek cheese plate on the table in Kukla's Kouzina follows, with details about each variety, their uses, and acceptable recipe substitutions (if available). Keep in mind that substitutions can alter a recipe's authentic flavor.

FETA (φέτα, FEH-tah)
(sheep's and/or goat's milk, aged and kept in a salty whey brine for at least two months)
White, soft-creamy to semi-firm crumbly, ranges from moderately salty to salty-peppery-sharp

The most famous Greek cheese, feta, cured and stored in its own salty whey brine, comes in as many varieties as there are towns in Greece, and a good number of these varieties are named for the region they come from. Most imported feta varieties are made from sheep's milk and have a rich, creamy texture. Some are made with goat's milk, which gives them a tangy quality—you'll even find little wheels of goat feta that are scored from being ripened in small baskets (kalathakia or kofinakia), as opposed to the usual rectangular blocks. A few are made with both sheep's and goat's milk, combining the qualities of each. If a cheese is labeled as feta but is made with cow's milk (a "domestic" variety in the United States) it is not real feta—it has none of the rich flavor or texture of traditional feta.

Always read the label and look for sheep's milk, goat's milk, or a combination of the two. Most specialty markets will let you have a taste to help you choose.

These are a few of our favorite feta varieties:

ARAHOVA (Αράχωβα, ah-RAH-hoh-vah)
(sheep's milk—semi-firm, sharp, a bit salty, peppery)
Great for baking in a pita, like spanakopita, and frying, as in *saganaki* (see *Food Terms*). Arahova is also good for crumbling in a salad or serving sliced with a drizzle of extra-virgin olive oil and kalamata olives.

BULGARIAN (Βουλγαρική, vool-yah-ree-KEE)
(sheep's and/or goat's milk—semi-firm, tangy, salty)
Best for baking and frying but also good for salads or serving sliced.

DODONI (Δωδώνη, thoh-THOH-nee)
(sheep's milk—firm, salty)
Good for baking, frying, salads, or serving sliced.

FRENCH: GALLIKI (Γαλλική, yah-lee-KEE)
(sheep's milk—soft to semi-firm, creamy, mildest of the feta family)
This feta is perfect for serving fresh in salads, crumbled in an omelet, or sliced on a meze plate.

GRAVIERA (γραβιέρα, ghrah-VYEH-rah)
(sheep's milk, sometimes combined with a small amount of goat's milk, aged at least five months)
Light buttery-yellow, semi-hard, firm, sweet, fruity, nutty, mellow, intense aroma

The highest quality graviera comes from Crete and is served sliced, alone or with *mezedes* (see *Food Terms:* Meze).

Substitution: manchego

HALLOUMI (χαλλούμι, hah-LOO-mee)
(sheep's milk)
White, firm, mild, moderately salty

This brined cheese comes from Cyprus and has an almost rubbery quality that softens but doesn't melt when heated. Halloumi cuts into perfect slices for frying, as in *saganaki* (see *Food Terms*), grilling, or dicing for a salad. Unlike most cheeses, halloumi can be refrigerated up to six months or frozen up to one year without harming its texture or flavor.

KASSERI / KASERI (κασέρι, kah-SEH-ree)
(sheep's milk alone or combined with goat's milk, made in the regions of Thessalia and Xanthi, and the island of Mitilini, aged over three months)
Light buttery-yellow, semi-firm, mild, creamy, salty-sweet, nutty

Wonderful as a sliced table cheese, or shredded/diced and tossed with hot pasta. You'll always find at least two cheeses on a Greek table, feta and kasseri. Kasseri is also the cheese used in Greece to make pizza.

Substitution: manchego

KEFALOGRAVIERA (κεφαλογραβιέρα, keh-fah-loh-ghrah-VYEH-rah)
(sheep's milk, sometimes combined with goat's milk, made in western Greece, aged at least three months)
Light buttery-yellow, hard, salty, nutty

As the name suggests, this cheese is a marriage between kefalotyri and graviera, merging the qualities of both to form a semi-sharp cheese ideal for grating over dishes, using in savory pitas, or making *saganaki* (see *Food Terms*).

Substitution: high-quality Parmigiano-Reggiano (not recommended for Saganaki)

KEFALOTYRI (κεφαλοτύρι, keh-fah-loh-TEE-ree)
(sheep's milk alone or combined with goat's milk, aged at least three months)
Light buttery-yellow, hard, sharp, salty, tangy, strong aroma

Perfect for grating over pasta or vegetables, in savory pitas, or garnishing cooked dishes.

Substitution: a half-and-half mix of high-quality Pecorino Romano and Parmigiano-Reggiano

MYZITHRA / MIZITHRA (μυζήθρα, mee-ZEE-thrah)
(sheep's and/or goat's milk, fresh)
White, unsalted, mild flavor, strong aroma, generally sold in round balls or loose by weight

A whey cheese made from feta and kefalotyri by-products, it makes a delicious topper for pastas, pizzas, stews, soups, and salads. It's also used as a filling in pastries and desserts.

  NOTE: Because this is a fresh unsalted cheese it is very perishable, so purchase no more than two days before using.

Substitutions: full-fat sheep's-milk ricotta
(If sheep's-milk ricotta is not available, use full-fat cow's-milk ricotta and drain overnight in a cheesecloth-lined colander set over a bowl in the refrigerator before using.)

MYZITHRA / MIZITHRA KSERI (μυζήθρα ξερή, mee-ZEE-thrah kseh-REE): DRY MYZITHRA
(sheep's and/or goat's milk myzithra, air-dried)
White, hard, heavily salted

Perfect for grating over pasta and vegetables. In the seaside town of Glifada in Athens, restaurants sprinkle it over french fries for an unbelievable side dish we call patates tiganites (πατάτες τηγανιτές, pah-TAH-tehs tee-ghah-nee-TEHS) or Greek fries.

Substitutions: dry-aged ricotta salata (pressed, salted, and dried ricotta), high-quality Pecorino Romano

For more on Greek cheeses, visit our website:
Feta Feast
Greek Cheese: Delectable Varieties & Uses

EGGS: AVGA (αυγά, ah-VGHAH)

In many of our recipes we use extra-large eggs. This is because the standard egg size that is used for cooking and baking in Greece is equivalent to extra large in the Untied States. Since the majority of these recipes come from our mother and grandmother, this is the only size they featured in their foods. They made generous batches of certain recipes for family gatherings or special occasions (like two hundred cookies for Christmas or a wedding), so in those cases our recipes were scaled down for the home kitchen in this cookbook series, occasionally making large eggs the best to use.

GARLIC: SKORDO (σκόρδο, SKOHR-thoh)

No matter how you slice, chop, crush, or mash it, garlic is a must when it comes to making the garlic sauce Skordalia (σκορδαλιά, skohr-thah-LIAH), slow-roasted lamb, lentil soup, and a ton of other dishes. In Greek cooking, it usually partners with lemon juice or vinegar, which balances out the flavor of each dish perfectly.

GRAPE LEAVES: KLIMATOFILLA (κληματόφυλλα, klee-mah-TOH-fee-lah) / AMBELOFILLA (αμπελόφυλλα, ahm-beh-LOH-fee-lah)

Grape leaves are used to make *dolmadakia* (see *Food Terms*; *Greek Cooking Techniques:* Dolmadakia: How to Prepare and Roll, page 45).

Grape leaves come brined in a jar and are widely available in Greek, Mediterranean, and specialty markets. Look for light-colored leaves, as these will be young and tender. If you have access to grapevines, again, choose the light green younger leaves—they'll be smaller than the dark ones, but you don't need large leaves for dolmadakia. May and June are the peak months for picking fresh young leaves.

HERBS: VOTANA (βότανα, VOH-tah-nah)

There are a number of herbs that are used specifically for Greek cooking and a few that are also used in other cuisines. Following are the herbs Greeks use most often. These are the essential Greek kouzina staples when it comes to Kukla's *mezedes* (see *Food Terms:* Meze). If you want to cook like a Greek, you have to stock up like one.

DILL: ANITHOS (άνηθος, AH-nee-thohs)

Greeks will only use fresh dill, as it looses much of its flavor when dried. This is the herb that gives the signature taste to the yogurt-cucumber sauce Tzatziki (τζατζίκι, tzah-TZEE-kee), the Pascha (Easter) lamb soup magiritsa (μαγειρίτσα, mah-yee-REE-tsah), and a feta-filled Greek omelet or omeleta (ομελέτα, oh-meh-LEH-tah). Add dill during the last minutes of cooking to retain its essence.

MINT: DIOSMOS (δυόσμος, thee-OHZ-mohs)

This herb is used fresh and dried, each imparting a very different taste and aroma to a wide array of dishes, including the classic herbed miniature meatballs Keftedakia (κεφτεδάκια, keh-fteh-THAH-kyah), the zucchini pie kolokithopita (κολοκυθόπιτα, koh-loh-kee-THOH-pee-tah), and the stuffed cabbage rolls lahanodolmades (λαχανοντολμάδες, lah-hah-noh-dohl-MAH-thehs).

OREGANO, GREEK: RIGANI (ρίγανη, REE-ghah-nee)

Greek oregano comes from the mountainsides of Greece and is known to control erosion. The name is taken from the ancient Greek *oros* (mountain) and *ganos* (joy), meaning *joy of the mountain.*

This herb is used fresh and dried. The dried version is sold ground, as well as on stems in bunches, the latter being the more preferable, aromatic form. Greek oregano is the most fragrant of all the oregano varieties and is the "Opa!" in Greek salads, roasted lamb dishes, Karpathian meat sauce, and sprinkled on feta slices with a drizzle of extra-virgin olive oil.

PARSLEY, FLAT-LEAF: MAINTANOS (μαϊντανός, maheen-dah-NOHS)

Like dill, only fresh will do. This antioxidant-loaded herb is rich in A, B, and C vitamins and is widely used in soups, sauces, and cheese fillings.

For more on Greek herbs, visit our website:
Greek Herbs, Spices & Flavorings

LEGUMES: OSPRIA (όσπρια, OHS-pree-ah)

Greek legumes (beans) come in a wide range of unique shapes and sizes, and are the protein-rich foundation of the Mediterranean diet. From ancient times to today's kouzina, they're considered the backbone of fasting and Lenten meals. In this book we feature versatile chickpeas.

CHICKPEAS / GARBANZO BEANS: REVITHIA (ρεβίθια, reh-VEE-thyah)

Revithia are used in mezedes (like houmous), soups, salads, stews, breads, vegetable side dishes, and main dishes.

Houmous me tahini (χούμους με ταχίνι, HOO-moos meh tah-HEE-nee): This is hummus made with *tahini* (see Tahini) and is simple to make using a food processor. Homemade is much healthier than store-bought, with less fat and more abundant chickpea flavor. We serve this spread as a meze or side dish with pita wedges, crackers, and vegetables. Variations we love to make include Sun-dried Tomato, kalamata Olive, and Artichoke and Spinach. These, as well as our original Lemon-Pepper Hummus recipe, are included in this book (page 15).

For more on legumes, visit our website:
Legume Kouzina

LEMON: LEMONI (λεμόνι, leh-MOH-nee)

Just about everything in Greek cooking has lemon in it and no self-respecting Greek would be caught dead without lemons in their refrigerator. It adds iconic tang to avgolemono soup, roasted chicken and potatoes, and custards. Lemons are to Greek cuisine as curry is to Indian food. You'll find lemon mostly combined with the other Greek essentials of olive oil, oregano, and garlic. Together, these four flavors can turn ordinary food into a Greek dish—poultry, fish, lamb, tomato salad, artichokes, sauces, and so many more foods get their signature taste from this tart citrus fruit.

For more on lemons, visit our website:
Lemon Lust

OLIVE OIL: ELEOLADO (ελαιόλαδο, eh-leh-OH-lah-thoh)

Eleolado, as we call it, basically translates from elia (ελιά, eh-LYAH), which is *olive*, and ladi (λάδι, LAH-thee), which is *oil*. Olive oil has been one of the most valued oils in Greece for thousands of years and is considered THE oil in the Greek kouzina, which is why it's simply referred to as ladi. Olive oil is irreplaceable in Greek cooking and is a key component of the Mediterranean diet.

Olive oil is categorized based on its degree of acidity. The lower the acidity, the more fruity and flavorful the oil. When you see "cold-pressed" on the label it means the oil was extracted from the olives using a chemical-free process (applying only pressure), producing a natural, low-acidity level. "Unfiltered" means that the oil did not undergo a filtering treatment, leaving tiny particles of olive fruit (the gist) in the oil, which translates into more flavor in the oil and less handling when it comes to processing—a purist's dream.

Following is a breakdown of the basic grades of olive oil.

EXTRA-VIRGIN OLIVE OIL, the cold-pressed, first pressing of the olives, has a 1 percent or less acidity level (the lowest acidity of all the olive oils). This is the fruitiest and most expensive olive oil so you wouldn't use it much for cooking (high heat/frying can break down the flavor, so it would be a waste), but it's the only oil you'd want to eat raw, like on salads, drizzled over cooked foods, and for dipping fresh, crusty bread into.

VIRGIN OLIVE OIL is also a first press oil but with a slightly higher acidity of 1 to 3 percent. Good for low- or medium-heat cooking (when you want the flavor of the olives in your food) and eating (though not as flavorful as extra-virgin).

FINO OLIVE OIL is an extra-virgin and virgin blend. Also good for low- or medium-heat cooking and eating.

LIGHT OLIVE OIL is lighter in color and olive flavor because it has undergone an extremely fine filtration process, which gives it a higher smoke point, making it ideal for high-heat frying. Because of its bland flavor, it's perfect for the kind of baking or cooking where a more flavorful olive oil would be overpowering. If you want the benefits of olive oil but not the rich taste, then this is the all-purpose oil for you.

OLIVE OIL or PURE OLIVE OIL is a blend of refined olive oil (chemicals are used to extract the oil from the olives) and virgin or extra-virgin. Not so "pure," huh? The chemicals are enough of a reason to stay away from this one.

Our Kukla's basic rule of thumb was "the darker green the color is, the better the olive oil will be." She was right of course! The deeper the color, the more intense the olive flavor, and if you're serving it at the table, go extra-virgin with the lowest acidity.

Extra-virgin Karpathian olive oil—fruity, low acidity (0 to 0.6), smooth light pepper finish, with notes of oregano, fig, and grapes—is our favorite, but unfortunately it's not available in the United States. Our search for a locally-sold favorite resulted in finding two olive oils that have won over our hearts. They're the only ones we use in our recipes and serve at the table—they make a noticeable and delicious difference. For cooking, we discovered olive oil from the island of Crete. Since Crete is a neighbor to Karpathos, it's not surprising that its oil is also similarly notable—0 to 0.8 percent acidity, cold pressed, unfiltered, extra-virgin—and available under a generic Crete label. For serving, family-owned Mentis Estate, located in the village of Neapolis in historical Laconia in Greece's southern Peloponnese, produces an exceptional extra-virgin olive oil. Olive oil from Laconia is made special by the uniquely flavorful Athenolia olives indigenous to that region, and Mentis Estate has been producing some of the area's finest extra-virgin olive oil for three generations—unblended, 0.3 percent acidity, aromatic, and fruity, with the well-balanced characteristics of pine, floral, nutty, and buttery, with a hint of artichoke.

In the end it really comes down to personal taste. To narrow down your choices, buy a small bottle and try it out. If you're happy with it, you can go back for a larger bottle or a can. If there's room for improvement, try a different one. Make it a tasty adventure of discovery and enjoy the journey to good food and good health.

> STORING: Store olive oil in a cool, dark place, like your kitchen cupboard (away from the stove/oven) for up to 6 months. If you use it often, you can buy a large can (which is less expensive than buying it by the bottle) and pour it into a stainless steel *olive-oil can/decanter* (see *Equipment:* Eleodoheo/Eleodoxeo) or a tinted bottle fitted with a spout (wine bottles are perfect; just wash them out first). That way you can refill the dispenser as needed and keep the bulk of the oil stored and protected.

For more on olive oil, visit our website:
Olive Oil: Branch to Bottle
Greek Olive Oil Varieties: Choosing and Cooking

OLIVES: ELIES (ελιές, eh-LYEHS)

Greek olives are not just about the renowned kalamata. They come in a vast assortment of colors, shapes, and sizes, as well as flavors. From brined to dry-cured, almond-shaped to oval, plain to herbed, pitted to stuffed to pureed, there are so many delicious varieties that boredom can't find a seat at *our* table.

An exclusive olive variety can be found in just about every region of Greece, with some varieties named after the region they're grown in. Following is a list of imported Greek olives that we enjoy and serve often with mezedes, in salads, and so much more.

AGRINIOU / AGRINION (Αγρινίου / Αγρίνιον, ah-ghree-NEE-oo / ah-GHREE-nee-ohn) are green, brine-cured, jumbo-size olives from Agrinio near Greece's west coast by the Ionian Sea. The Agriniou olive's firm, juicy flesh is effortlessly removed from the pit, making them easy to eat or use in recipes. Once brined, these fruity olives are lightly coated with extra-virgin olive oil, and tossed with oregano, slices of fresh lemon, and crushed whole garlic cloves. They're also available with a coating of hot red-pepper flakes.

AMFISSA (Άμφισσα, AHM-fee-sah) and HALKIDIKI / CHALKIDIKI (Χαλκιδική, hahl-kee-thee-KEE) are green, brine-cured, large or jumbo-size olives that are stuffed with almonds. They come from Amfissa near the ancient city of Delphi and Halkidiki/Chalkidiki in northern Greece. They're picked when very large in size (to accommodate the stuffing), then slowly brined, producing a fruity and mild olive with a crisp skin and meaty flesh. The pits are replaced with whole blanched almonds for an irresistible spin on the plain olive...or the plain almond, for that matter.

KALAMATA (*Καλαμάτα*, kah-lah-MAH-tah) are light- to deep-purple, brine-cured, almond-shaped olives that come in medium, large, and jumbo sizes. The most famous of all of the Greek olives comes from the Kalamata region on the southwestern side of the Peloponnese peninsula. These olives are protected under the European Union and they must be from this area and harvested from the Kalamon tree in order to be called "kalamata," so beware of labels like "kalamata-style" or "kalamata-type" as they will not be the real thing. Authentic kalamata olives can also be labeled "PDO Kalamata," which refers to the olive's Protected Designation of Origin (the PDO label is used on other Greek olive varieties as well).

Kalamata olives are smooth, tight-skinned, and meaty, and are imparted with a richly unique fruit-wine flavor from the addition of red wine or red-wine vinegar to the brine during the curing process. These olives also come pitted for easy serving in salads, baking in breads, or pureeing for homemade olive spread.

> Which brings us to OLIVE PASTE / SPREAD, Pasta Elias (*πάστα ελιάς*, PAH-stah eh-LYAHS). The most common is a deep-purple tapenade made purely from kalamata olives, though green-olive spreads are also available. Flavored with a dash of lemon juice and oregano, it's ideal for spreading on crackers or bread as a meze, or for use as a topping on fish and vegetables. (Our recipe is on page 16.)

KOULOUMBOTES (*κουλουμβότες*, koo-loom-BOH-tehs) from Karpathos are black, dry-cured, small olives that are especially fruity and sweet, as well as tender. Kouloumbotes can be found growing in most Karpathian villagers' backyards (including ours) and are served at every taverna on the island. These are the little olive gems every visitor raves about.

NAFPLIO / NAFPLION (*Ναύπλιο*, NAHF-plee-oh) are green, brine-cured, small to medium-size almond-shaped olives from Nafplion on the eastern coast of the Peloponnese peninsula. They have a crisp, firm texture, and a faintly smoky, nutty flavor. Nafplio olives are available plain, spiced with coriander seeds, or coated with extra-virgin olive oil and herbs, with slices of fresh lemon and crushed whole garlic cloves.

THASOU / THASSOU (*Θάσου*, THAH-soo) are black, dry-cured, small to medium-size olives that come from the island of Thasos/Thassos in the northern part of the Aegean Sea. This olive is a bit larger than the famed Moroccan, with a smaller pit that makes this variety meatier.

For more on olives, visit our website:
Olive Kouzina

PHYLLO: FILLO / FILO (*φύλλο*, FEE-loh)
The Greek word for leaf or sheet is phyllo or fillo, as in the thin sheets of pastry dough used in *mezedes* (see *Food Terms:* Meze) like Mbourekia, savory dishes like tyropita, and sweets like baklava. Phyllo comes in a number of sheet thicknesses, as well as in shredded and pre-baked shell forms.

In the previous chapter, *Greek Cooking Techniques:* Phyllo (Fillo/Filo), page 43, we talked about how to work with phyllo, and here we'll get acquainted with the vast array of phyllo-dough products so you can simplify your choices and get cooking. The three major phyllo brands that feature these products are Athens/Apollo, Kontos, and The Fillo Factory—these are the most widely available in U.S. markets and online.

SHEET NUMBERS AND SIZES
The number on the phyllo-sheet boxes refers to the thickness of the sheets of dough. The lower the number, the thinner and more delicate the sheet, and the flakier the result. The thicker the sheet, the easier it is to work with but the less flaky it will be, and you'll need to use more butter and/or olive oil to keep the phyllo from becoming hard while baking.

Phyllo sheets come in different sizes as well: 9-by-14-inch (for mini pans or mezedes, like individual triangles or rolls), 12-by-17-inch (for small pans), and 14-by-18-inch (for large pans). When making a large pita, if you can't find the bigger sheets, you can use a smaller size and overlap them by one inch to line the bottom of the pan and cover the top of the pita, brushing with butter and/or oil in between the seam to seal in place.

Following is a phyllo breakdown, including sizes, descriptions, uses, and baking results for each. (See *Greek Cooking Techniques:* Phyllo (Fillo/Filo): How to Work with It, page 43, for tips.)

#4 / #5 THIN PHYLLO DOUGH Intermediate to experienced bakers, but beginners can also have success
All-purpose, tissue thin, silky, delicate, and pliable. This phyllo requires a light touch with a natural-bristle pastry brush to avoid tearing.

Best for everything, including mezedes (like Tyropitakia Triangles or meat-filled Mbourekia rolls), entrées (like spanakopita), and dessert pastries (like nutty flogeres).

Bakes up soft, light, flaky, and golden in color.

Sizes: 9-by-14-inch, 12-by-17-inch, 14-by-18-inch

#7 THICK PHYLLO DOUGH Beginner to experienced
Thicker and easier to work with than #4, this phyllo is still flexible but not as tender or flaky. With #7 you'll use fewer sheets than #4 but you'll need to apply a more liberal coating of butter and/or olive oil onto each sheet.

Best for large entrées (like hortopita, a leafy-greens pie) and pan syrup-desserts (like custard-filled galaktomboureko). The thicker #7 phyllo may also be used to make individual-sized mezedes.

Bakes up slightly flaky, crisp, and golden in color.

Size: 14-by-18-inch

#10 EXTRA-THICK COUNTRY STYLE (HORIATIKO) PHYLLO DOUGH All experience levels
This is the thickest phyllo and the least flexible. With #10 you'll use fewer sheets than #7 but you'll need to apply an ample coating of butter and/or olive oil to each sheet.

Best for large entrées and country-style savory pitas (like melitzanopita, an eggplant pie), pan syrup-desserts (like baklava), and strudels. The thick #10 phyllo also works well for en papillote–style (in parchment) fish recipes, making the entire dish edible.

Bakes up crunchy and golden brown in color.

Size: 14-by-18-inch

SHREDDED PHYLLO DOUGH: KATAIFI (κατάϊφι, kah-tah-EE-fee) All experience levels
Because it's shredded, kataifi can be formed into a number of shapes, including shells, nests, and cones. You can roll it, layer it, fold it, or wrap it.

Best for party foods, mezedes, entrées, and festive desserts (like nut or custard rolls). Layer it in traditional dishes (replacing the phyllo sheets) for a distinct texture and appearance.

Bakes up crunchy with golden strands.

Size: 16 ounces

PHYLLO SHELLS, MINI / LARGE All experience levels
Preformed and baked (located in the freezer section of your market), these shells are ready to use right out of the package for fast and easy serving.

Best for party foods, mezedes, salads, entrées, and desserts.

Bake up crisp. Baking is not required so you can use these shells for cold salads, puddings, or anything that's ready to serve. If baking, first brush the shells with olive oil before filling and placing in the oven.

Sizes: 15 mini or 6 large

For more on phyllo, visit our website:
Fillo (Phyllo): Learn How to Work with It and Bake Beautifully

RICE: RIZI (ρύζι, REE-zee)
The following five basic types of rice most commonly used in Greek cooking are comprised of translucent, pearly whites (similar in appearance to Arborio) and pale-yellow to brown hues, with sizes ranging from medium to long grain. One rice does not fit all recipes, so choose wisely.

GLASSÉ (γλασσέ, ghlah-SEH, meaning *glossy*)
(white short-to-medium-grain rice)
This rice has a shiny coating and is best for soups like magiritsa (Pascha/Easter lamb soup) and desserts.

CAROLINA (*Καρολίνα*, kah-roh-LEE-nah)
(white medium-grain rice)
This is a flavorful, starchy rice that's best for risotto and desserts like rizogalo (rice pudding).

NYCHAKI (νυχάκι, nee-HAH-kee, meaning *little fingernail*)
(white long-grain rice)
The longer grain makes this rice best for rice dishes, pilafs like spanakorizo (spinach with rice), and salads.

KITRINO (κίτρινο, KEE-tree-noh, meaning *yellow*)
(parboiled or converted white long-grain rice that has turned a pale yellow after processing)
This rice cooks up tender but firm, holding its shape, making it best for stuffings, as in *dolmades* (see *Food Terms*), stuffed tomatoes and peppers (see *Common Cooking Methods:* Gemista/Yemista), as well as pilaf and rice side dishes.

KASTANO (καστανό, kah-stah-NOH, meaning *chestnut colored*)
(brown rice)
This rice can be used as a substitute for white or yellow rice in many recipes to add healthy fiber to a meal.

For more on rice and grains, visit our website:
Grain Kouzina

SEA SALT: THALASSINO ALATI (θαλασσινό αλάτι, thah-lah-see-NOH ah-LAH-tee)
Amazing food requires high-quality ingredients—fresh vegetables, choice meats, and, *yes*, sea salt. In Kukla's Kouzina, as in Greece, this is the only salt we use. Our number one reason is its natural salt-water flavor (instead of the harsh chemical taste of table salt). Sea salt also dissolves more easily than table salt when cooking.

Sea salt is usually not processed, or undergoes minimal processing, and therefore it retains trace levels of minerals like magnesium, potassium, calcium, iodine, and other nutrients. The minerals add flavor and color to sea salt, which also comes in various grain grades and crunchy textures. The final result is a delicate brine taste and pleasant mouthfeel. It's a noticeable difference.

Greek sea salt comes in fine, medium, and coarse crystals, and is inexpensive compared to sea salts of other origins. A wonderful pantry addition for those with artisanal tastes is fleur de sel from Laconia, Greece (from Mentis)—the ultimate flavor enhancer that finishes a dish perfectly. For flavored, flaked sea salt with an added dimension of crunch, we look to Cyprus, whose epicurean varieties are infused with essences like wild garlic and citron.

For more on sea salt, visit our website:
Sea Salt: Cook, Taste, Savor
Sea Salt: Meze to Dessert Recipes

SESAME SEEDS, IVORY: SOUSAMI / SISAMI (σουσάμι, soo-SAH-mee)

Sesame enhances a number of our foods, making it another kouzina staple we can't live without. We use it as a topping for breads (savory and sweet), Karpathian psilokouloura (twisted breadsticks), and cookies like koulourakia, and it's the main ingredient in the wedding sweet sousamomelo/sisamomelo that is bound with honey. Sesame is also ground into a paste to make *tahini* (see Tahini).

SESAME SEEDS, BLACK: MAVROSOUSAMO / MAVROSISAMO (μαυροσούσαμο, mah-vroh-SOO-sah-moh)

These small black sesame seeds impart a nutty, smoky, oregano-peppery flavor to recipes. The most common use is sprinkling them on breads, kouloures (bread rings), and breadsticks, alone or combined with the more common ivory-colored sesame.

SPICES: MBAHARIKA (μπαχαρικά, mbah-hah-ree-KAH)
ALLSPICE: MBAHARI (μπαχάρι, mbah-HAH-ree)

This pea-sized berry of a West Indian evergreen tree (*Pimenta dioica*) of the Myrtle family embodies the flavors of cinnamon, nutmeg, and cloves, hence the name. Though sold in dried-berry and ground form, it's best to grind the berries as needed for the freshest taste. A pinch goes a long way in tomato-based sauces, meats, and Karpathian breads.

CLOVE: GARIFALO (γαρίφαλο, ghah-REE-fah-loh)

This dried, unopened flower bud of a tropical evergreen tree (*Syzygium aromaticum*) of the Myrtle family is an essential spice worldwide. Clove's aromatic, peppery flavor lends itself to a number of dishes from sauces and meats to desserts like karidopita (walnut cake with syrup), cookies like kourambiedes (shortbread cookies dusted with confectioners' sugar) and ahladakia amigdalota (almond pears), as well as spoon sweets.

NUTMEG: MOSCHOKARIDO (μοσχοκάρυδο, mohs-hoh-KAH-ree-thoh)

This dark-brown seed from an evergreen tree (*Myristica fragrans*) of the Myristicaceae family, native to the Spice Islands, is a lighter brown to tan color on the inside and has a warm, spicy-sweet taste. Though you can use it pre-ground, for the most aromatic and flavorful addition to your foods, we suggest you grate it fresh when you need it (you *will* notice the difference). This spice can be found in béchamel sauce (used in moussaka and pastitsio), potato croquettes, syrups, and cakes.

For more on Greek spices, visit our website:
Greek Herbs, Spices & Flavorings

TAHINI (ταχίνι, tah-HEE-nee)

Tahini consists of hulled sesame seeds that have been toasted and ground into a smooth paste. This is the main ingredient in dips like Hummus as well as Lenten sweets like tahinopita (ταχινόπιτα, tah-hee-NOH-pee-tah), also called tahini cake. Delicious and high in protein on its own, many Greeks use it as a spread on toast instead of butter. Tahini is sold plain, with added honey, and flavored with chocolate.

TARAMA (ταραμά, tah-rah-MAH)

Tarama is the coral-colored, tiny-egg roe of carp and is considered a type of caviar. This roe is ground in a wooden *goudi* (see *Equipment*) and then used as the main ingredient in the dip/spread Taramosalata (ταραμοσαλάτα, tah-rah-moh-sah-LAH-tah). The tarama is what gives the dip its attractive coral hue.

VANILLIN: VANILIA (βανίλια, vah-NEEL-yah)

Vanilia is a crystalline form of vanilla that is extracted from the bean, and is the only vanilla used in Greek baking because it is the most aromatic and flavorful component of the vanilla bean. It's white in color, looks a bit like confectioners' sugar, and is made up of tiny crystal flakes. The flavor is extremely concentrated compared to vanilla extract, so a very small amount is used—a pinch usually does the trick. It imparts a pure vanilla essence to recipes without the aftertaste of alcohol (from the extract) making it perfect for pastries, custards, cakes, pitas, cookies, and breads. It's a bit pricey but remember that a little goes a *very* long way, and it makes Greek desserts taste like heaven, just the way they were meant to.

For more on Greek flavorings, visit our website:
Greek Herbs, Spices & Flavorings

WINE AND SPIRITS: KRASI KAI LIKER (κρασί και λικέρ, krah-SEE keh lee-KEHR)

Greek wines are among the finest produced today and are the perfect companion to any cuisine, especially Greek. The liqueurs used most commonly in Greek cooking and baking are brandy/cognac (κονιάκ, kohn-YAHK) and ouzo (ούζο, OO-zoh). Metaxa is Greece's iconic brandy, aged five (5 Star), seven (7 Star), and 12 (12 Star) years. We use the less expensive 5 Star for our recipes and reserve the 12 Star for after-dinner cocktails. Ouzo is a robust, anise-flavored liqueur that has achieved worldwide recognition as *the* Greek drink. Ouzo can be used in recipes as well as for sipping—add a couple of ice cubes to your glass and watch this colorless liqueur turn cloudy. The essential anise oil in the liqueur dissolves in alcohol but not in water, producing what scientists call the Ouzo Effect.

For more on Greek wines and spirits and food pairings, visit our website:
Greek Wine & Food Pairing
Greek Spirits, Dessert Wine & Sweets Pairing

YOGURT: GIAOURTI / YIAOURTI (γιαούρτι, yiah-OOR-tee)

Greek yogurt is naturally thick, creamy, mild, and sweet. In Greece it's usually made from sheep's milk, which is the reason it displays these characteristics. Greek yogurt is used to make the yogurt-cucumber sauce Tzatziki, as well as an amazing syrup-drenched yogurt cake known as giaourtopita (γιαουρτόπιτα, yiah-oor-TOH-pee-tah). It's also simply served drizzled with honey, sprinkled with walnuts, and topped with fresh fig wedges. Homemade drained yogurt is an acceptable substitute for Greek yogurt when cooking or baking (see *Greek Cooking Techniques:* How to Make Greek Yogurt, page 46).

COMMON COOKING METHODS

A few basic cooking methods are used in the Greek kouzina, and the dishes themselves are often named after the method used to prepare them. These method terms are included in recipe titles to add emphasis to the style of cooking used. It immediately tips off the cook as to how the dish will taste and how to make it. The flavor combinations in Greek cooking methods are what define this ethnic cuisine and make it so unique and beloved. Below you'll find the methods of Greek cooking used in this book, along with examples of foods we prepared in these styles.

AVGOLEMONO (αυγολέμονο, ah-vghoh-LEH-moh-noh)

Avgo (αυγό, ah-VGHOH) is *egg* and lemono/lemoni (λεμόνι, leh-MOH-nee) is *lemon*, so avgolemono is a mixture of egg and lemon that is added to stock to make avgolemono sauce or soup. Avgolemono sauce is customarily poured over *dolmades* (see *Food Terms*), giouvarlakia (meatballs with rice similar to the dolmades stuffing), and vegetables. Avgolemono also goes well with chicken, as is shown in avgolemono soupa (αυγολέμονο σούπα, ah-vghoh-LEH-moh-noh SOO-pah), a chicken soup that contains rice or orzo.

GEMISTA / YEMISTA (γεμιστά, yeh-mee-STAH)

Gemista means *stuffed* and refers to all foods that are prepared this way. The stuffing is usually made of ground meat, rice, tomato, and flavorings. Once filled, the dish is then cooked. The meze recipes in this book that use this method include Stuffed Mushrooms or Gemista Manitaria (γεμιστά μανιτάρια, yeh-mee-STAH mah-nee-TAH-ryah) and Stuffed Grape Leaves known as Dolmadakia me Klimatofilla (ντολμαδάκια με κληματόφυλλα, dohl-mah-THAH-kyah meh klee-mah-TOH-fee-lah) (see *Food Terms:* Dolmades, Dolmadakia).

MBOUREKI(A) (μπουρέκια, mbou-REH-kyah)

Mboureki(a) refers to a food that is rolled in phyllo or homemade dough and then baked, like our Mbourekia me Tyri (μπουρέκια με τυρί, mboo-REH-kyah meh tee-REE), Cheese Rolls, and Mbourekia me Kima (μπουρέκια με κιμά, mboo-REH-kyah meh kee-MAH), Meat Rolls.

NISTISIMA / NISTISIMO (νηστίσιμα, nee-STEE-see-mah)

Nistisima/nistisimo means *for fasting* or *Lenten* and is a classification used for all foods prepared without meat or meat products, making them appropriate for Lent. These foods are also considered vegan and usually include olive oil, vegetables, and grains. Kukla was quite resourceful when it came to combining ingredients to make a delicious Lenten meal. One of those dishes is featured in this book—Dolmadakia Gialantzi-Nistisima (ντολμαδάκια γιαλαντζί-νηστίσιμα, dohl-mah-THAH-kyah yiah-lahn-DZEE nee-STEE-see-mah), or Lenten Stuffed Grape Leaves.

SFOLIATA (σφολιάτα, sfoh-LYAH-tah)

Sfoliata is *puff pastry* and refers to foods baked in this flaky dough, such as our Spanaki Sfoliata (*σπανάκι σφολιάτα*, spah-NAH-kee sfoh-LYAH-tah), Spinach Puffs, and Elia Sfoliata (*ελιά σφολιάτα*, eh-LYAH sfoh-LYAH-tah), or Olive Puffs.

FOOD TERMS

Following are terms that relate to Greek food, including those that apply to recipes in this book.

DOLMADES (ντολμάδες, dohl-MAH-thehs)

Greek dolmades (from the Arabic dolma, meaning *something stuffed*), come in two forms, grape leaf and cabbage. The stuffing ingredients and seasonings vary from region to region in Greece, and in the Middle East they may look like their Greek cousins but it's the use of local spices, flavorings, nuts and/or fruit that sets them apart.

DOLMADAKIA (ντολμαδάκια, dohl-mah-THAH-kyah) are small dolmades made with *grape leaves: klimatofilla/ambelofilla* (see *Ingredients*) and filled with a ground lamb and/or beef-and-rice stuffing. Dolmadakia made with rice alone are called Dolmadakia Gialantzi (*ντολμαδάκια γιαλαντζί*, dohl-mah-THAH-kyah yiah-lahn-DZEE), and, because they're meatless, can be served during Lent or fasting periods. They're also referred to as *nistisima* (see *Common Cooking Methods*), meaning *for fasting*. Both dolmadakia versions are traditionally served as *mezedakia* (see Meze) with lemon wedges. (See *Greek Cooking Techniques:* Dolmadakia: How to Prepare and Roll, page 45.)

For more on dolmades/*dolmadakia*, visit our website:
Greek Dolmades: Stuff, Wrap & Roll

ELLINIKOS KAFES (Ελληνικός καφές, eh-lee-nee-KOHS kah-FEHS)

Ellinikos (Greek) kafes (coffee) is the classic demitasse made with a powder-fine grind. The coffee, sugar, and cold water are combined in a *briki* (see *Equipment*), then brought to a boil to form a creamy foam called *kaimaki* (see Kaimaki). The kaimaki and half of the coffee are divided among the demitasse cups—this is to ensure that each cup has kaimaki. The remaining coffee in the briki is then returned to a boil and divided once again among the cups, filling them to the brim. Once poured, the coffee is not stirred so the grounds can properly settle to the bottom. When it's cool enough to drink, the flavorful coffee is sipped until the muddy grounds are reached (the grounds are discarded). In Greek homes, offering Ellinikos kafes is a sign of hospitality and is always served with a glass of water and a sweet like biscuits or cookies.

To make a medium or *metrios* (*μέτριος*, MEH-tree-ohs) coffee: for each demitasse cup of water, stir in ½ teaspoon of sugar and 1 heaping teaspoon of coffee.

HOUFTA (χούφτα, HOOF-tah)

A houfta is a *handful*, as in mia houfta alevri or *one handful of flour*. As with much of Greek cooking, this vague measuring method is just one of many passed down through the generations, like one wineglass or a tea cup, as you'll see explained throughout this section. Since everyone's hand size is different, the recipe can be affected. Also, one houfta can be heaping with the palm mostly open while another can be just the amount that fits in a nearly closed fist. An experienced cook knows his or her way around a kitchen by feel with no need for a written recipe. We sat our mom down and had her bring her measurement vessels (including her hands) to the table, then filled them and emptied them into a measuring cup. What a difference between her houfta and ours!

KAFENIO (καφενείο, kah-feh-NEE-oh)

Kafes (see Ellinikos kafes) is *coffee*, lending its name to kafenio, the local *coffeehouse* where the men go to have their Greek demitasse, play cards or backgammon (*τάβλι*, TAH-vlee), and talk about politics, news, or football (soccer)—basically shooting the breeze. It's the original man-cave.

KAIMAKI (καϊμάκι, kahee-MAH-kee)

This is the prized creamy foam, similar in appearance to espresso crema, that forms at the top of *Greek coffee* (see Ellinikos kafes) while being made in a *briki* (see *Equipment*). If the kaimaki does not form or is minimal, it could mean that not enough coffee was used, the coffee was not properly brewed, the grind was too coarse, or the coffee was stale.

KALI OREXI (καλή όρεξη, kah-LEE OH-reh-ksee)
"Kali orexi" means *good appetite*—or as the French would say, "Bon appétit." This is the term we use as a toast before a meal, and it's how Kukla signed off on each of her handwritten recipes.

KILO (κιλό, kee-LOH)
Kilo is *kilogram*, a common Greek weight measurement: 1 kilo equals 1 pound 3.3 ounces.

KOUZINA (κουζίνα, koo-ZEE-nah)
This is the *kitchen*, the heart of the home. It's where all the magic happens—so it's no wonder that this is where everyone gravitates when guests are invited. Why hang out in the living room when you can witness the good stuff unfolding right before your eyes and under your nose before it's even plated? If the heart of *your* home turns into a full house, be a smart hostess by delegating tasks to your kouzina visitors—it'll get you away from the hot oven quickly so you can spend more time enjoying the party!

KUKLA / KOUKLA (κούκλα, KOO-klah)
Kukla is the Greek word for *doll* and is used as a term of endearment to describe a beautiful woman. Our mom, Mary, called the girls she loved at work "Kukla." They adored her and affectionately called her "Kukla" in return. The name stuck—and it didn't take long before we all started calling her Kukla. Since our Kukla was a Greek *gourmet* goddess, we decided it was the perfect name for this cookbook series, a collection of her most treasured and loved recipes.

LADERA (λαδερά, lah-theh-RAH)
Ladi (λάδι, LAH-thee) is *oil*, so ladera refers to a classification of foods that are oil-based and, for the most part, vegetarian, like Lenten Stuffed Grape Leaves or *Dolmadakia Gialantzi* (ντολμαδάκια γιαλαντζί, dohl-mah-THAH-kyah yiah-lahn-DZEE) (see Dolmadakia; *Common Cooking Methods:* Nistisima). These peasant dishes are timeless and the meatless versions are ideal for Lent.

MATSAKI (ματσάκι, mah-TSAH-kee)
Matsaki means *a small bunch*, and is usually used in reference to herbs like parsley or dill.

MEZE (μεζέ, meh-ZEH) / plural: MEZEDES (μεζέδες, meh-ZEH-thehs)
Meze is a little plate of food that can be a snack, an appetizer, or a tasting. On a meze platter you'll find everything from *mezedakia* (mini bites) like Dolmadakia, Keftedakia, and Tyropitakia, to dips or spreads like Taramosalata, Tzatziki, and Melitzanosalata.

OKA (οκά, oh-KAH)
Another common Greek weight measurement, 1 oka is equal to about 1.280 kilos or 2.8 pounds.

OREKTIKA (ορεκτικά, oh-reh-ktee-KAH)
Orektika—from the Greek word orexi (όρεξη, OH-reh-ksee, see Kali orexi), meaning *appetite*—are appetizers that can be less substantial than mezedes or just as hearty. They can consist of olives, cheese, sliced deli meats, stuffed eggs, shrimp, canapés, crackers and spreads, and/or croquettes. Orektika come in hot and cold varieties and are meant to usher in a meal, like Italian antipasto. Mezedes are more filling and can stand on their own. Many times these two terms are used interchangeably.

OUZERI (ουζερί, oo-zeh-REE)
This is where *ouzo* (see *Ingredients:* Wine and Spirits) is served, along with brandy, wine, and all manner of libations. It's Greece's version of a bar, *taverna* style (see Taverna). An ouzeri is basically an extension of a taverna, providing a full bar, as well as serving food.

PITA (πίτα, PEE-tah) / plural: PITES (πίτες, PEE-tehs)
Pita brings to mind pita bread, but in actuality, pita is a savory or sweet pie made in a large tray lined and topped with phyllo or dough. Examples of a savory pita would be spanakopita (spinach pie), and a sweet pita would be galaktomboureko (a custard-filled pie drizzled with syrup). When several pites are made in individual mini-size forms, like triangles and rolls, you'll see the suffix "kia," as in spanakopitakia (little spinach pies). Pita also refers to a cake or bread, like Vasilopita (Saint Basil's/New Year's cake or bread).

POTIRAKI (ποτηράκι, poh-tee-RAH-kee)

Potiraki is a *small juice glass*, also used as a Greek measuring vessel. No two potirakia are the same and each home chef has her own set of glasses she uses to cook and bake with, so your friend's recipe might not work in your kouzina unless you happen to have the same drinkware.

POTIRI (ποτήρι, poh-TEE-ree)

Potiri is a *large drinking glass*. Potiri nero (ποτήρι νερό, poh-TEE-ree neh-ROH) is a *large water glass*, and potiri krasiou (ποτήρι κρασιού, poh-TEE-ree krah-SYOO) is a *wineglass*. All three glass sizes are in the Greek cook's pantry for both drinking and measuring.

PREZA (πρέζα, PREH-zah)

Preza is a *pinch*, as in a pinch of salt. This could mean anything from a few grains to ¼ teaspoon. It's important to sit down with the cook and ask them what their version of a preza is before trying to make one of their recipes.

SAGANAKI (σαγανάκι, sah-ghah-NAH-kee)

Saganaki is a *skillet/frying pan*, usually cast-iron, used to make a number of dishes that include the skillet's name in the recipe title, like garides saganaki (shrimp saganaki). The most popular of these recipes is the appetizer simply called Saganaki, which is slices of Greek cheese—usually *feta, halloumi, kasseri,* or *kefalograviera* (see *Ingredients: Cheese: Tyri*)—that are fried in a skillet until crisp on the outside and soft on the inside. Liqueur is added to create a flame just before serving, though a flameless version is a comparable opition. Once plated, lemon is squeezed over the top and simple cheese is transformed into a distinctively Greek meze.

STIN IGIA SAS (στην υγειά σας, steen ee-YAH sahs)

Stin igia sas means *"To your health!"* and is said as a toast before having a drink (like "Cheers!"). It's used when addressing a group or a person you should show respect to. Stin igia sou (στην υγειά σου, steen ee-YAH soo) is the more casual term used when speaking to a close friend or family member. Gia sas (γειά σας, YAH sahs) and gia sou (γειά σου, YAH soo) are shortened versions that are also used when someone sneezes or for saying "Hello" and "Good-bye" (like "Ciao").

TAVERNA (ταβέρνα, tah-VEHR-nah) / plural: TAVERNES (ταβέρνες, tah-VEHR-nehs)

The taverna is the classic Greek eatery with outdoor seating in most places. Arches of grape vines, carafes of retsina (a resin-flavored Greek wine), and platters overflowing with *mezedes* (see Meze) create the ambiance of Mediterranean bliss when a meal with good company is in order. There's a limited bar menu at a taverna, so if you want more of a selection, choose an *ouzeri* (see Ouzeri).

> NOTE: In English, the plural of taverna is referred to as tavernas, whereas in Greek it's more accurately called *tavernes*.

To learn more about the eateries in Karpathos, visit our website:
Tavernas & Restaurants of Karpathos

GREEK FOOD & PRODUCT SOURCES

Following is a list of our favorite markets, websites, and products that will give you a number of easy ways to purchase ingredients and equipment, taking the stress of shopping out of your meal preparation.

Greek products are readily available in Greek and Mediterranean markets, specialty stores, and are sometimes carried in supermarkets in Greek neighborhoods. If you don't know of a market near you, we suggest contacting a Greek church or organization in your area and asking if they know of any markets nearby.

GREEK / MEDITERRANEAN MARKETS IN NEW YORK
If you're in New York, these are the ultimate Greek foodie shops to visit (you can also call them to ask if they have the items you're looking for and if they can ship them to you):

Mediterranean Foods (2 locations)

22-78 35th Street	30-12 34th Street
Astoria, NY 11105	Astoria, NY 11103
718-721-0266	718-728-6166

www.mediterraneanfoodsny.com

Sahadi's
187 Atlantic Avenue
Brooklyn, NY 11201
718-624-4550
www.sahadis.com

Titan Foods
25-56 31st Street
Astoria, NY 11102
718-626-7771
www.titanfoods.net

CHEESE
Mediterranean Foods stores (Astoria, NY) and online, www.mediterraneanfoodsny.com (locations above)
Sahadi's store (Brooklyn, NY), www.sahadis.com (location above)
Titan Foods store (Astoria, NY), www.titanfoods.net (location above)
Limited varieties:
Amazon, www.amazon.com (search for "Greek cheese" or specific cheeses, Grocery & Gourmet Food section)
Costco, select stores (Dodonis feta), www.costco.com (for locations)
igourmet.com, www.igourmet.com
Whole Foods Market stores, www.wholefoodsmarket.com/stores/list (for locations)

FOODS, NONPERISHABLE
Hellenic Farms, www.hellenicfarms.com
Mediterranean Foods stores (Astoria, NY) and online, www.mediterraneanfoodsny.com (locations above)
My Cretan Goods, www.mycretangoods.com
Recipiada, www.recipiada.com (Greek Supermarket section)
Titan Foods store (Astoria, NY) and online, www.titanfoods.net (location above)

OLIVE OIL FROM GREECE
Mediterranean Foods stores (Astoria, NY) and online, www.mediterraneanfoodsny.com (locations above)
Mentis Estate extra-virgin olive oil, www.mentisestate.com
Sahadi's store (Brooklyn, NY) and online, www.sahadis.com (location above)
Titan Foods store (Astoria, NY) and online, www.titanfoods.net (location above)

PHYLLO (FILLO / FILO)

Amazon, www.amazon.com (Grocery & Gourmet Food section)
Athens/Apollo Fillo Dough, supermarkets, Greek markets, www.athensfoods.com (for stores)
Kontos Fillo dough, Greek markets, www.kontos.com (contact for stores)
Mediterranean Foods stores (Astoria, NY), www.mediterraneanfoodsny.com (locations on previous page)
Sahadi's store (Brooklyn, NY), www.sahadis.com (location on previous page)
The Fillo Factory, www.fillofactory.com
Titan Foods store (Astoria, NY), www.titanfoods.net (location on previous page)

SEA SALT

Amazon, www.amazon.com (Grocery & Gourmet Food section)
Falksalt (Crystal Flakes sea salt from Cyprus), www.falksalt.com/us
Mediterranean Foods stores (Astoria, NY) and online, www.mediterraneanfoodsny.com (locations on previous page)
Recipiada, www.recipiada.com (Mentis Fleur de Sel sea salt)
The Spice Lab (sea salt flakes from Cyprus), www.spices.com
Titan Foods store (Astoria, NY), www.titanfoods.net (location on previous page)

SPICES, HERBS, FLAVORINGS, COFFEE, AND TEA

Greek Internet Market, www.greekinternetmarket.com
GreekShops.com, www.greekshops.com
Kouzounas Kitchen, www.kouzounaskitchen.com
Loose Leaf store (28-10 23rd Avenue, Astoria, NY 11105) and online, www.shoplooseleaf.com
Mediterranean Foods stores (Astoria, NY) and online, www.mediterraneanfoodsny.com (locations on previous page)
Parthenon Foods, www.parthenonfoods.com
Sahadi's store (Brooklyn, NY) and online, www.sahadis.com (location on previous page)
Titan Foods store (Astoria, NY) and online, www.titanfoods.net (location on previous page)

WINE AND SPIRITS

Omega Wines & Spirits
23-18 31st Street
Astoria, NY 11105
718-726-0056
www.omegawinesandspirits.com

Shop from Omega's website or call for information on in-store special events and wine tastings. Stop by for a visit the next time you're in the area and revel in their amazing Greek selections—they'll be happy to recommend a wine for your next occasion. Mention "Kukla's Kouzina" and get 10 percent off your purchase!

EQUIPMENT

Amazon, www.amazon.com (10- to 17-inch metal skewers, Grilling & Barbecue Utensils section)
Fante's Kitchen Shop, www.fantes.com (*plastis*/rolling pins; *gastra*/clay bakers; olive oil can)
GreekShops.com, www.greekshops.com (*tapsia*/trays, pans; stainless steel *briki*/Greek demitasse coffeepot; olive oil can/dispenser)
Mediterranean Foods stores (Astoria, NY), www.mediterraneanfoodsny.com (*briki*; *tapsia*) (locations on previous page)
Parthenon Foods, www.parthenonfoods.com (squash cleaner/corer; copper, stainless steel, and enamel *briki*; demitasse cups; brass and marble *goudi* and *goudoheri*/mortar and pestle; *tapsia*)
Recipiada, www.recipiada.com (*briki* and demitasse cups, Accessories section)
Titan Foods store (Astoria, NY), www.titanfoods.net (*briki*; *tapsia*) (location on previous page)

INDEX

a
artichoke and spinach hummus, 15
avgolemono, stuffed grape leaves, 40-41

c
canapés, ham, 37
carp (fish) roe spread, *14*, 19
cheese, 48-50
    fried Greek, flambé, *32*, 33
    meat rolls, 29
    olive puffs, *24*, 25
    pies with homemade dough, mini, 26-27
    rolls, 28, *29*
    spinach puffs, 22-23
    stuffed mushrooms, 36
    triangles, phyllo, 30
chickpea(s), 52
    hummus
        artichoke and spinach, 15
        lemon-pepper, *14*, 15
        olive, 15
        sun-dried tomato, 15
cocktail meatballs, *38*, 39
cooking methods, common Greek, 58-59
    avgolemono, 58
    gemista (yemista), 58
    mbmoureki(a), 58
    nistisima/nistisimo, 58
    sfoliata, 59
cooking techniques, Greek, 43-46
    dolmadakia, how to prepare and roll, 45-46
    how to make Greek yogurt, 17, 46
    phyllo (fillo/filo), how to work with it, 43-45
    using a *goudi* and *goudoheri* (mortar and pestle), 46
cucumber, yogurt- sauce/dip, 17, *38*

d
dip (see also *sauce* and *spread*)
    garlic, *skordalia*, *14*, 18
    hummus, *houmous*
        artichoke and spinach, 15
        lemon-pepper, *14*, 15
        olive, 15
        sun-dried tomato, 15
    yogurt-cucumber, *tzatziki*, 17, *38*
dolmadakia (dolmathakia, ντολμαδάκια), 59
    gialantzi-nistisima (γιαλαντζί-νηστίσιμα), 42
    how to prepare and roll, 45-46
    me klimatofilla (με κληματόφυλλα), 40-41
dough
    homemade, mini cheese pies with, 26-27

e
egg(s), 51
    ham canapés, 37
    Kukla, 28
    -lemon sauce, stuffed grape leaves, 40-41
eggplant-salad spread, *14*, 20
elia sfoliata (ελιά σφολιάτα), *24*, 25
equipment, Greek, 47-48

f
fillo/filo (see *phyllo*)
fish (see *seafood*)
food terms, Greek, 59-61
fried Greek cheese flambé, *32*, 33

g
garides me saltsa kokteil (γαρίδες με σάλτσα κοκτέιλ), 34, *35*
garlic sauce/dip, *skordalia*, *14*, 18
gemista manitaria (γεμιστά μανιτάρια), 36
goudi and *goudoheri*, 47, how to use, 46
grape leaves, 41, 51
    dolmadakia, how to prepare and roll, 45-46
    stuffed, 40-41
    stuffed, meatless-Lenten, 42
Greek shrimp cocktail, 34, *35*

h
ham canapés, 37
herbs, 51
houmous (χούμους), 52
    me aginares kai spanaki (με αγκινάρες και σπανάκι), 15
    me elies (με ελιές), 15
    me lemoni kai piperi (με λεμόνι και πιπέρι), *14*, 15
    me liasti ntomata (με λιαστή ντομάτα), 15
hummus
    artichoke and spinach, 15
    lemon-pepper, *14*, 15
    olive, 15
    sun-dried tomato, 15

i
ingredients, Greek, 48-58

k
kanape me zampon (καναπέ με ζαμπόν), 37
Karpathos, 1-3, *6*, 7-10, 27, 48, 51, 53, 54, 57, 61, 67

olive puffs, *24*, 25
spinach puffs, 22-23

keftedakia (*keftethakia*, κεφτεδάκια), *38*, 39
kouzina, 1, 60
Kukla, 1-5, 60

l

legumes, 52
    hummus
        artichoke and spinach, 15
        lemon-pepper, *14*, 15
        olive, 15
        sun-dried tomato, 15
lemon-pepper hummus, *14*, 15
Lenten stuffed grape leaves, meatless-, 42

m

mb014reki(a) (μπουρέκι/μπουρέκια), 58
    me kima (με κιμά), 29
    me tyri (με τυρί), 28, *29*
meat
    ham canapés, 37
    rolls, 29
    stuffed grape leaves, 40-41
meatballs, cocktail, *38*, 39
meatless-Lenten stuffed grape leaves, 42
melitzanosalata (μελιτζανοσαλάτα), *14*, 20
mini cheese pies with homemade dough, 26-27
mortar and pestle, 47, how to use, 46
mushrooms, stuffed, 36

n

nistisima, dolmadakia (*dolmathakia*) *gialantzi-*, 42
nut(s), walnuts, stuffed mushrooms, 36

o

olive(s), 53-54
    hummus, 15
    paste/spread, *14*, 16
    puffs, *24*, 25
olive oil, 52-53

p

pasta elias (πάστα ελιάς), *14*, 16
phyllo (fillo/filo), 54-56
    cheese rolls, *mbourekia me tyri*, 28, *29*
    cheese triangles, *tyropitakia trigona*, 30
    how to work with it, 43-45
    meat rolls, *mbourekia me kima*, 29
pies, mini cheese with homemade dough, 26-27
pork, ham canapés, 37
potato(es)
    carp (fish) roe spread, *taramosalata*, *14*, 19
    garlic sauce/dip, *skordalia*, *14*, 18
preparation, food, 11
puffs/pastry
    olive, *24*, 25

spinach, 22-23

r

rice, 56
    stuffed grape leaves, 40-41
    stuffed grape leaves, meatless-Lenten, 42

s

saganaki (σαγανάκι), *32*, 33, 61
sauce (see also *dip* and *spread*)
    avgolemono, stuffed grape leaves, 40-41
    béchamel, cheese rolls, 28
    cocktail, Greek shrimp cocktail, 34, *35*
    garlic, *skordalia*, *14*, 18
    yogurt-cucumber, *tzatziki*, 17, *38*
seafood
    carp (fish) roe spread, *taramosalata*, *14*, 19
    shrimp cocktail, Greek, 34, *35*
sfoliata (σφολιάτα)
    elia (ελιά), *24*, 25
    spanaki (σπανάκι), 22-23
skordalia (*skorthalia*, σκορδαλιά), *14*, 18
spanaki sfoliata (σπανάκι σφολιάτα), 22-23
spice(s), 57
spinach
    hummus, artichoke and, 15
    puffs, 22-23
spread (see also *dip* and *sauce*)
    carp (fish) roe, *taramosalata*, *14*, 19
    eggplant-salad, *melitzanosalata*, *14*, 20
    olive paste, *pasta elias*, *14*, 16
stuffed grape leaves, 40-41
stuffed grape leaves, meatless-Lenten, 42
stuffed mushrooms, 36
sun-dried tomato hummus, 15

t

taramosalata (ταραμοσαλάτα), *14*, 19
tomato
    cocktail sauce, Greek shrimp cocktail, 34, *35*
    eggplant-salad spread, *14*, 20
    hummus, sun-dried, 15
tyropitakia (τυροπιτάκια), 43-44, 55
    me spitiko fillo (με σπιτικό φύλλο), 26-27
    trigona me fillo (τρίγωνα με φύλλο), 30
tzatziki (τζατζίκι), 17, *38*

v

vanillin, *vanilia* (βανίλια), 57

y

yogurt, 58
    -cucumber sauce/dip, 17, *38*
    Greek, how to make, 17, 46

ABOUT THE AUTHOR & THE TEAM

KELLY SALONICA STAIKOPOULOS

Kelly Salonica Staikopoulos is the author and editor of the cookbook series *Kukla's Kouzina: A Gourmet Journey~Greek Island Style*, as well as a recipe developer and tester, and the website mistress and blogger for *kuklaskouzina.com*. Kelly is also a cohost on *Kukla's Kouzina's* YouTube cooking channel.

Kelly has been a contributing food editor and writer for fifteen years, working with a number of national publications, including *Ladies' Home Journal*, *Working Mother*, and *Reader's Digest*. She has developed recipes and written food articles for *Woman's World*, *Ladies' Home Journal*, *richmondnavigator.com*, *Chesterfield Living*, and *West End's Best*, and has been featured as a radio personality reporting on food trends for *WHAN's The Flav~Feeding Trendzy* in Richmond, Virginia. Kelly is also a travel and entertainment writer whose articles have appeared in *American Way*, *Country Weekly*, *Ladies' Home Journal*, *backstage.com*, *countrystandardtime.com*, and *Chef's Edge* (Chefs de Cuisine Association of America).

Kelly's artistic talents are clearly inherited from her mother, Mary (Kukla), and proudly displayed in her paintings, sketches, and of course food styling, which she provided for this cookbook's photography. Kelly is also an actress and worked on Netflix's *Crime*, CBS's *Person of Interest*, the CW's *The Carrie Diaries*, NBC's *Law & Order*, and *The Amazing Spider-Man 2*.

JOANNE STAIKOPOULOS MARZELLA

Joanne Staikopoulos Marzella is a recipe developer and tester for *Kukla's Kouzina: A Gourmet Journey~Greek Island Style*, as well as the business manager for this project. Joanne is also a cohost on *Kukla's Kouzina's* YouTube cooking channel.

Joanne is married with a daughter and two stepsons. She spent the bulk of her professional life as an Executive Vice President and Chief Financial Officer in the advertising/media field, where her client base included Toys"R"Us, Tyco, Mattel, Milton Bradley, and Pressman. Seventeen years ago, when she and her husband Vincent had their daughter, she embarked on a new career as mother and role model for little Jacqueline Maria.

Joanne's focus is now on enriching her child's life with the roots of her Greek heritage, of which her grandma Mary's culinary treasures and memories are certainly an important part. Joanne's stepsons, Matthew and Daniel, adored Kukla and have always embraced her way with food. While both enjoy eating, Daniel takes it one step further by rolling up his sleeves and whipping up a few Greek dishes of his own. Suffice it to say, when Kukla's dishes are on the dinner menu, there isn't an empty seat at the table!

JACQUELINE MARIA MARZELLA

Jacqueline Maria Marzella is a graduate of the Young Chefs Academy in New York, making her a valuable asset to our test kitchen. She just graduated high school with honors and is a competitive swimmer. Formerly on a high-ranking team in New York, she held the position of captain of her high-school swim team. She also enjoys singing, dancing (especially Greek dancing where she competes), and acting—she participated in all her school plays, codirected the middle-school productions, and will be studying theater in college this fall.

Jackie cooks alongside Kelly and Joanne, and also joins them as a cohost on *Kukla's Kouzina's* YouTube cooking channel. There are many Greek foods Jackie loves to make, but two stand out on her list of favorites: bread (our *yiayia* Kalliope's *Christopsomo* recipe) and Christmas cookies (our Kukla's *melomakarona/finikia*, *kourambiedes*, and *koulourakia*).

Early training in the kitchen combined with coming together to share in the making of these family recipes have instilled in us a deep appreciation of our heritage and of one another's innate abilities. The camaraderie, the respect, the teamwork, and the love forged in this longstanding family tradition have built the foundation on which we all rely to keep us grounded as we move forward, while keeping our Kukla's legacy alive!

ABOUT KUKLASKOUZINA.COM

The heart of our cookbook and website is the passing on of our customs and culinary history to the next generation in a fun and engaging way, securing the legacy started by our mom and grandmother while encouraging our children to be as inventive as they were.

Our BLOG, *The Naked Truth About…Greek Cooking!*, is all about traditional Greek food from the island of Karpathos and serves as a companion to our cookbook series, *Kukla's Kouzina: A Gourmet Journey~Greek Island Style*. In our posts are Greek cooking techniques and tips that demystify what is sometimes considered a complicated cuisine, which will help you re-create the dishes of the gods in your very own kitchen. We also talk about specialty ingredients used in Greek cooking and tell you where you can buy them, as well as offer any acceptable substitutions. In addition to food, we explore Karpathian culture and music to turn your journey into a well-rounded experience.

Our VIDEOS page features cooking demonstrations that pair with our recipes. In our GALLERY you can view a slide show of our foods; then take a trip down memory lane with Kukla, from her early years growing up, to her life at work and play; and finally take a peak at the next generation.

We welcome you to go to our CONTACT US page to submit your comments, questions, and requests. This is where you can also sign up for our e-newsletter. We'd love to help you take your own journey~Greek island style!

Our mom's ultimate lesson to us, and now to you, is: *Never settle for ordinary when you can create something extraordinary!*

VISIT AND CONTACT US ONLINE AT WWW.KUKLASKOUZINA.COM